How to Build a Real Estate Brand

The 4 Step Guide to Build a Successful Real Estate Brand Strategy, Marketing and Development of Real Estate Brand

Damian McMillan

CONTENTS:

Introduction:

Branding has evolved in recent times as a corporate strategy. In addition to the product-related brands, all business organizations and industries adopted the strategy of creating their identity through brands. Branding is certainly a tool for advertising. Branding is the way to connect and identify customers with your business.

The key to good visual brand identity is to make sure it is well-defined, cantered, unique, impactful, and, most importantly, memorable. You may think branding is a good method for selling commercial products, but your real estate business will benefit from many of the same benefits. Real estate brands with a strong and consistent name differentiate themselves from the competitors. Customers will only buy a service from a company they trust, because on some distrusted basis, no one will ruin their precious time and money. Branding will help you build trust value in the clients ' hands. Whether you are new to the market or have a well-recognized brand, the creation and differentiation of real estate brands are vital steps and essential components of your overall marketing strategy for real estate and home builders. You need to evaluate the market now that you have a good idea of your target audience, and what abilities and strengths you need to give them. The business is said to have established brand equality once a product has generated positive sentiment among its target audience. A brand is a cumulative influence or lasting impression of everything that consumers who meet a company or its products and services can see, hear, or experience.

This book demonstrates why brand development is important in real estate business, all the marketing strategies and guidelines to mentor your business in digital media to make it successful, and the idea of creating a brand name in the market to express a lifestyle and part of the high-end residential property sales strategy. This book is about to read the hands-on process of creating a successful brand, maintaining brand value, and Marketing improvements.

Chapter 1: How to Build a Successful Brand

A brand is a sign, tag, image, title, term, or phrase used by companies to differentiate their product from others. For creating a brand identity, a combination of one or more of these elements can be useful.

A trademark is called legal protection is given to a brand name. Brands vary from products in such a way that brands are "what consumers buy," while products are "what concerns/companies do." The product is an aggregation of associations of emotion and purpose. The brand is a promise that the product fulfills the expectations of the customer. It shapes the expectations of the customer regarding the product. Brands typically have a mark that protects them from being used by others. A brand offers corporate, product, or service data that differentiates it from others on the marketplace. The brand has an assurance of the features that make the product or service unique. A strong brand is a way to make people aware of what the product is about and its purpose. Brands simplify the purchase decision for consumers. Consumers can discover the products that meet their needs over some time.

When customers understand and have an awareness of a brand, they make a quick purchase decision and save a lot of time. We also save the price of the consumer quest. Consumers stay committed and to a brand if they believe and get an implicit understanding that the brand will continue to meet their standards.

If consumers receive benefits and satisfaction from the product's consumption, they will continue to purchase that brand more likely. Brands also have a critical role to play in convincing customers of specific product features. It's important to remember when creating a brand, whether you're online or offline, is consistency. In all media, you must be the same — be relevant, be true, and be genuine to who you are. People can spot a scam from a mile away, which does not bode well when dealing with the most significant investment of most customers. So, be precise in who you are and what consumers can expect from the experience. From the quest to post-close follow-up, the client experience should be smooth and consistent. Part of creating and preserving that continuity is to build a team of people who you regularly work with and that are part of your trusted brand. People who are (you) loyal to a brand are more likely to try another brand (your colleagues) services. These colleagues may include mortgage brokers, lawyers, or moving companies who may also be involved in the transaction's seamlessness. Developing the brand to include these service providers not only means that your customer is well cared for now, but also when they decide to return for round two in the future. Friends and colleagues are going to ask each other, "Are you a good agent? "You want to say yes to them and mention your name afterward. You required potential buyers and sellers, on the experience and product they can trust, as quickly as you make your choice between coffee and tea-based on their branding.

1.1 Creating a Brand

When a company chooses to settle on a brand, they first need to determine their brand identity, and how people consider that brand. A company logo, for instance, also incorporates the company's message, slogan, or product. The aim is to make the product memorable and consumer-friendly. The company usually consult with a design firm or design team to develop ideas for a brand's visual aspects, such as the logo or symbol. A right product accurately portrays the thought or feeling that the company is trying to get across and contributes to brand awareness or acknowledgment of the presence of the brand and what it provides. On the other hand, lack of communication often results in an ineffective brand.

The business is said to have established brand equity once a product has generated positive sentiment among its target audience. A few examples of brand equity companies— with highly recognizable consumer names — are Microsoft, Coca-Cola, Toyota, Apple, and Twitter. If done correctly, a brand leads to higher sales not only for the specific product that sold but also for other products sold by the identical company. A good brand increases trust in the customer, and the consumer is more likely to try another product similar to the same brand after having a great experience with one product. This phenomenon also refers to as brand loyalty. Branding is the way to connect and identify customers with your business. Your branding at a high level is made up of the design elements that separate you from your competition. For example, the name, logo, and slogan of your company are very distinctive of who you are. Branding, though, goes far deeper than that. Through every single touchpoint, it remains essential. You can even make the use of color, fonts, photographs, and the quality of the printed material.

Regardless of size, most business owners want their company to create a name. A brand is a cumulative influence or lasting impression of everything that consumers who meet a company or its products and services can see, hear, or experience. You must control the impact that product or service has on the customer by creating a brand or "branding." We're going to look at the hands-on process of creating a brand and what it can mean as a shareholder. The product is your customer's pledge. It tells them what they can assume from your products and services that distinguish your bid from that of your rivals. The identity comes from who you are, who you want to be, and who you believe you are.

1.2 Why Branding is Essential

Branding is essential to a company because of its overall impact on your business. Branding can change the way consumers view the product, can drive new business, and increase brand awareness. Because it is how a company gets attention and becomes recognizable to customers, the reason is branding is essential to a business. The logo is the essential element of branding, particularly concerning this factor, as it is essentially the company's face. That's why professional logo design should be
strong and easy to remember, making a first glance impression on a person. Printed promotional products are a way to communicate this.

Branding is important when trying to attract future business, and by giving the company more influence in the market, a well-defined brand will increase the value of a business. That makes it a more attractive investment opportunity due to its firmly established marketplace position. There will be no problem with a distinctive brand to drum up the referral business. Branding means that customers have a positive impression of the product, and they likely to do business with you due to the perceived consistency of using a name that they can trust. Once a brand is well known, word of mouth will be the best and most effective marketing strategy for the business.

Branding is something that occurs when all these elements are put together and commercialized. By using carefully designed images, beautiful videos, and print materials, deeply thought-out advertising creates a cohesive vision that uniquely connects to your company through customers. By creating a recognizable and memorable experience for them, it sets you apart from the others.

You will build trust and drive authority by developing a likable brand for your business, as well as building loyalty with your customers. You will be able to reap all these benefits by correct brand positioning and attain higher prices and repeat business for your services. Developing a brand is one thing, but the key to a successful (and profitable!) brand identity is to apply it clearly and consistently across all of your media. You will work to strengthen the brand identity by using our iconic and influential marketing elements such as professional photography, videos, and print content. Likewise, if your marketing materials or print media don't suit your brand identity, you'll create a dissonance in your customers' minds.

It is important to ensure that your customers' visual touchpoints are in line with the expectations of your business. Such visual touchpoints are everywhere in the world of real estate. We are available on feature sheets handed out at properties in listing images seen on MLS. They are present in the quality of property video production, and the signage of the property listing. Many small companies are making the mistake of ignoring marketing efforts because they see themselves as a company rather than a brand. Brands, they say, with huge budgets and national recognition, are the big fish in the pond. Small businesses plans do little more than come up with a subtle logo and some colorful business cards, resigned to their supposed status as small-fish.

But for businesses of all sizes, branding is important because it increases their value, gives direction and motivation to employees, and makes it easier to acquire new customers. If a company professionally presents itself, and there is evidence that its products and services are reliable, people will trust in spending hard money.

Although your logo should not be all your branding efforts, you should still put effort into coming up with a memorable logo that professionally designed. Not only your logo must be significant, but this also gives your company's desired impression so that people think and feel what you want to believe. Marketing is a key part of your product. The chosen media and platforms, as well as the targeted audiences, help build the brand. Be aware that a promotional emphasis is too limited, or you risk being "pigeon-holed" and losing the ability to expand into new markets. Then again, too large an advertising emphasis could lead to your company being unable to create a definable impression in the minds of consumers. Anyone can hire staff, but only a strong brand can hire committed workers to bring your dream and mission forward. If you feel proud of your company, your employees do the same. It is important for employee morale and efficiency to have a strong brand.

Branding is one of the methods to do business with referral or word-of-mouth. And again, it's critical for your brand, branding, and credibility to work together to create an indelible impression on the minds of consumers. Think about it, if you can't remember the name, you can't tell your friend about the impressive golf clubs that you just purchased.

Good advertising generates a positive impression in your consumers ' minds and makes you stand out from your rivals. A branding investment will pay off in several ways.

• Increase mind sharing –You think of Coca-Cola or Pepsi when you want a soda. Kleenex comes to mind when you need a tissue. Are you in your market segment at the top of your account? Printed materials ' tactile components touch readers on an emotional level, linking consumers to your product in a way that cannot suit digital advertising. Imagine adding a gloss varnish, embossing, a distinctive die-cut, or one of the many textures in papers and other substrates that are now available.

• Create loyalty–A memorable experience with a quality brand builds loyalty, which results in the probability of again purchases and increases the likelihood that the consumer will buy related items from the same company.

• Referral benefits–People who have never used your product or service may still recommend it if they have had enough time to develop a sense of familiarity with your brand. For the casual observer, printed collateral can be more visible as the prospect does not need to search for your message consciously. Be sure to include information about your printed products on social media.

• Command a premium price–Effective branding can remove your product or service from the scope of a commodity, so buyers are keen to pay more for what you sell. Several companies are selling coffee, so what makes people stand up and pay Starbucks top dollars?

• Lower your advertising costs in the long run–although you need to spend resources to create a strong brand, you can sustain it once it is built without having to tell your story again. Most budget-conscious advertisers are heavily dependent on electronic media, but research shows that people still prefer printing. We just don't have the same visceral reaction as a professionally printed piece to an e-brochure.

• Less product threat leads to more revenue for you—If someone is put on the spot to decide, the brand name supplier will most likely be selected. Consider the monthly advertising of postcards so that prospects frequently connect with your product. Printed materials have an advantage over portable and permanent electronic media.

1.3 What do Brands do?

The Brand that has become a cult with many communities is proving to be a way of life. Knowing the power of the brands over the loyal customer community, the organizations have carefully nurtured and grown the brands in terms of their reputation and influence. Many successful brands are associating and supporting many social causes and promoting their social responsibilities. It has now become famous for the well-known brands to support sports, cultural, or music, as well as events related to business, and to align the brand with the specific field with which they affiliated. Branding has a partnership that is hugely successful.

You will soon realize when you analyze the brands and their associations that the brands represent a lot more than just the logo and the visual image. The visual representation is undeniably one of the brand's inherent attributes, but the products often express a perception associated with the image. In addition to having a personality, they have a distinctive role as well as importance and image. Examine a little further into the concept of branding, and you will find that the brands also acquire individual personalities. What we mean to answer is that the brands are the representatives of well-known celebrities. The brand ambassador's personality and public image also contribute to the image and popularity of the brand. Every personal item today, whether it is a fragrance or a watch, is synonymous with a well-known personality that reflects and promotes the brand. Mr. Richard Branson may be one of the most famous brand ambassadors and a brand in his own right. There are so many highly successful individuals, as well as actors and actresses representing and promoting and popularizing brands.

All in all, several different things are conveyed to different people by brands. Today, most successful companies are embracing their corporate identity or corporate brand to retain, preserve, and develop their public image of the company while continuing to promote their products on an individual basis. In such cases, we see that corporate branding and promotions attempt to communicate a different set of messages to customers while product brand promotions convey a completely different message. The corporate branding helps to cultivate and maintain the company identity, ideals, and reputation while the advertising introduces the product and its value proposition to target customers at the consumer level.

They are considering the different types of advertising that give us considering that the brands hold an influence that can be paired with an image as representation. In contrast, the company also carries a lot of elements and messages that it aims to express. Overall, you'll even notice that the brands have the power to access and stay in the viewers ' subconscious mind. They use this power, more importantly, to help the viewer as well as the customers to initiate and strengthen the relationship. Once you notice everything about brands around you, you will know that for different purposes, there is a development and strategy which goes into creating and those brands. This marks the origin of an interesting journey into the brand power world for students in marketing management.

It's not just competition about getting your target market. It's also about getting your prospects to see you as the only solution provider to your problem or need. Branding is, in fact, a problem-solver. A good brand will: deliver a message clearly Confirm the credibility of the brand on the marketplace Connect target prospects emotionally with a product or service Motivate the buyer to make a purchase Create user loyalty Effective branding can promote recognition for your business. If your brand is consistent and recognizable, it can help people feel more about buying from you in the east. People adhere to familiarity, and if you are remembered as a quality provider, you will be encouraged to repeat business as they are more likely to re-select your product or service. Branding is one of any business's most important aspects, large or small, retail, or B2B. In increasingly competitive markets, an effective brand strategy gives you a major edge. But what does "branding" mean exactly? How does a small business like yours affect it?

Simply put, your brand is your customer's promise. This shows them what they can expect from your products and services and distinguishes your bid from that of your rivals. Your brand originates from who you are, who you want to be, and who you feel you are. Are you the industry's creative maverick? Or the reliable and experienced one? Is your product the option that is high-cost, high-quality, or low-cost, high-value? You can't be both, and to all people, you can't be all things. Who you are, to some extent, should be based on who your target customers want and need to be?

Your brand is based on a logo. Your website material, packaging, and promotions, all of which should include your logo, should communicate with your brand. Your business brand strategy is how, what, where, to communicate and deliver brand messages. It's part of your brand strategy that you advertise. The channels of distribution are part of your brand strategy, as well. And your brand strategy also includes what you communicate visually and verbally. Consistent, strategic branding directs to strong brand equity, meaning the added value brought to the products or services of your company that enables you to charge more for your brand than the identical, unbranded command of products. Coke vs. a generic soda is the most obvious example of this. Since Coca-Cola has established strong brand equity, they can charge more for their product— and customers are going to pay the higher price.

In the form of attachment, the added value inherent in brand equity often occurs. Nike associates its products with star athletes, for example, hoping that customers will transfer their emotional attachment from the athlete to the product. Determining Your Brand is like a self-discovery business journey. It can be hard, time-consuming, and uncomfortable; it requires you to answer the following questions:
• What is the mission of your company?
• What are your products or services ' benefits and features?
• What does your business already think of your customers and prospects?
• What are the characteristics you want the organization to identify with?
Do the research you are doing. Learn about your current and prospective customers ' needs, habits, and desires. And don't rely on what they think you do. Know what they're thinking.

Because it can be hard to identify the brand and establish a marketing plan, consider using the resources of a Small

Business Development Centre or a non-profit advisory group.

How do you get the word out after you have identified your brand? Here are a few simple tips:

• Get a great logo. Place it all over.
• Write down your message about your brand. What are the fundamental messages about your brand that you want to communicate? That employee should be aware of the qualities of your brand.
• Create your brand. Branding encompasses every part of your business— how you respond to your mobile, what you or your salespeople wear on sales calls, your signature address, everything.
• Create a "voice" that reflects your brand for your company. This voice should be implemented to all written communication and embedded in the online and off visual imagery of all materials. Is it friendly to your brand? Be interested in the conversation. Is this an elegant thing? Be more formal than that. You're getting the gist.
• Setting up a tagline. Write a memorable, meaningful, and concise statement capturing your brand's essence.
• Design templates for your marketing materials and establishes brand standards. Use the same color scheme, place the logo, look, and feel all over. You don't have to be consistent, just fancy.
• You must be true to your brand. If you can't deliver as per your brand promise, customers won't come back to you— or refer you to someone else.
• Be consistent with each other. I've just put this last point because it's all about the above and the most valuable tip I can send you. If you can't do this, it will fail your attempts to set up a brand.

The workers will work aimlessly without direction. Obviously, this can create major issues for your company, so obviously it's something you'd rather avoid as often as possible. By creating a brand mission statement and direction, your employees will know where you're going and how they fit into the picture and will be able to do their job much more effectively.

To workers as well, this form of branding is very motivating. If you have a specific strategy in place and the team knows about it, they're going to know what to do, they're going to want to succeed, and they're going to do whatever it takes to achieve the organization's goals and take a business to the next stage.

Whether you're looking for new live chat technology or trying to improve some part of your business, it's going to help you get there. It will help the workers see the bigger picture, and they are going to take their duties much more seriously now that they know the game.

Believe it or not, you're going to start getting more referrals very quickly when you have a strong brand in place. It shouldn't come to anyone either as a major shock because people like to tell their friends, colleagues, and family members about their favorite brands and the businesses they like the most. Now, it's up to you to create a strong enough product that people love to talk to family and friends about. Through approaching your business this way, you won't have trouble attracting referrals and leads from your clients through word-of-mouth advertising, which is certainly something you'll enjoy because word-of-mouth referrals are the best marketing — and it's free too.

Consistency and consistency are important to share with the world while designing your branding post. If done correctly, your clients will know what you and your company are all about, and they will be able to determine if your business suits them properly. Through doing it this way, you'll make your customers feel relaxed because they know what your company is all about, they know what to expect, and if you're consistent with your message and consistently deliver the same products and services, your customers will feel confident they'll get. What they want and need when they buy from your website.

Finally, you and what you stand for are reflected by your name. You will be able to tell the world who you are very simple when you do it right, and they will have a much better idea of what your business is all about. Ideally, at this stage, you see the value of building a strong brand — the reasons why this is necessary for your business success. I have clearly stated. And, if you haven't already, start taking steps to grow your brand and start sharing a consistent message with your prospects and start booming in no time.

1.4 Brand Name Building

Many companies are motivated by a variety of ideas for developing products and services that can sell locally or internationally. These products or services need a brand or company name to be created. Such labels often include both logo and lettering and can make a great deal of publicity for such products or services. One of the steps in building a brand, therefore, is to decide on a brand name for the product or service that you want to sell.

Branding is a process that enables an individual or a group of individuals to provide an idea with a brand image and lettering. In doing so, one has a greater chance of selling these products to a wider audience, be it locally or internationally. Therefore, while the adage "nothing happens until someone sells it" still holds true to some extent, often, it almost seems as if the marketing and branding cycle has overtaken the selling intention.

While branding generally identifies the company behind it and its philosophies, it can also be representative of those who work for such a company. This is a positive thing because it creates the right kind of market to sell the product or service based on personal relationships with those running the business. Therefore, helping both the branded product or service selling organizations and the dealers purchasing the same.

One of the most important steps in the sale of any product or service is one's trust in the object. Therefore, only those who believe strongly in the company's products and services will be good at selling the same. Otherwise, when it comes to marketing at the same time, one might want to work from an advertisement or graphic artist perspective in relation to ads rather than sales. Another move is to build a brand with a good customer service department that retains loyalty to its customer base. For it can be a rare find to have such a department in today's world where one is both skilled and competent in supporting others. Thus, companies that represent themselves are often more successful than those that do not have a strong customer base and stronger customer service department.

In marketing a brand, a very important step is to identify the target audience before creating the marketing logo and lettering, different age groups react differently to a variety of logos and lettering, especially since a variety of gangs and others use such material inappropriately misrepresent so much. Therefore, if you can identify the brand name, logo and lettering and present the same to a review panel for marketing research or the like, you can gain a better understanding of which audience you need to target your product or service to in order to create the most sales. Nonetheless, if one can clearly communicate the use of their product or service, create trust within the group, whether locally or internationally, strive for marketing to the right audience, build a base of customers and customer loyalty and provide great customer service, then one is on its way to creating and advertising not only an excellent brand but also to selling one.

Therefore, when searching for steps to develop a brand, there are many steps that can be taken to help make it easier to construct such a product. These include understanding your market, creating your brand, having a great logo and lettering to reflect the same, targeting the right audience, and putting as many ads in as many online and offline marketing platforms as you can find. And after doing so, you might find that they're selling even more products and services than you ever dreamed possible. A powerful, reliable brand can make it possible for the consumer to know what to expect every time they meet your company. A professional appearance can create creditworthiness and trust, which bodes well as people are more likely to buy from a company that seems legitimate. You may not see a lot of success without proper and effective branding, no matter how good the marketing techniques may be, and how good the company itself may be.

Word of mouth is perhaps the best advertising tactic for any company, and it is certainly also the most effective. If a close one recommends it to you, you are more likely to buy a product or service than an advertisement. That's what healthy advertising does. It subconsciously creates an impression in the minds of your customers and helps build confidence and connection between them and your company. This makes them more likely to refer to people as your brand already looks so much better!

1.5 Maintaining Brand Value

Branding has evolved in recent times as a corporate strategy. In addition to the product-related brands, all business organizations in all industries adopted the strategy of creating their identity through brands. Branding is certainly a tool for advertising. The strategy of investing in brand building and managing the corporate brand's reputation goes beyond marketing, however. Branding is known to be a policy-driven and handled by the CEO or company in coordination with senior management and marketing heads. In recent years, we see the coining and calculation of new concepts of brand value, brand power, and brand equity, etc. If marketing professionals found it difficult to explain the product promotional behavior and get fines, they don't have to worry anymore today. Brand value and brand building costs have become a part of the balance sheet acknowledged. Brand value capitalization and brand marketing costs are budgeted and accounted for in the balance sheets, and in many instances, a brand's ROI is also estimated to reflect the level of product value over time.

In recent times, brand management has been gaining popularity. The fact that we have global brands well-established for over 50 years continues to prove the reality that brands have the power to make or break in the markets. Goodyear, Coco-Cola, Gillette, Nestle, Schweppes, Brooke bond, etc. have long been around and have developed enough brand power to manage growth through brand reputation and customer relationships.

Marketers realized the growing power of brands and began to promote the brand image through brand ambassadors and cultivate interest. Many fashions and luxury brands internationally and locally have as brand ambassadors' well-known actors and sportspeople etc. The advertisers derive the power to communicate with customers and create brand loyalty through the brand ambassadors ' persona. It also calls for the acceptance of the brand power to work on product quality and constant improvement in both the product and the promotion of brand ambassadors. Creating and increasing strong brand worldwide requires brand awareness for the entire organization. Apple is the best example of creating and understanding powerful brand power and unleashing brand value. You're right if you think the whole world outside is an Apple fan. But they also worship their brand within the entire organization. All policies, decisions, and day-to-day business decisions at all levels are aimed at promoting and strengthening the Apple brand. The whole company trusts in the brand and is motivated to develop the brand and offer superior customer experience through the brand through all business processes. Apple may be the best example of a successful corporate brand as a global brand.

In both the market and the balance sheets of the company that owns the brand, products have a certain quality. This is an issue the industry has agreed on. The brand value accounting and the brand value estimation approach are widely discussed. It becomes a strategic decision when companies pay a huge premium or goodwill to acquire a product. Nevertheless, accounting for the premium paid is a concern that many in the industry are addressing and debating.

There is no question that accountants would like to allocate a tangible value to each product owned by the company and the brand value charged for purchasing a brand, and the company is also considered an asset. One of the strategies adopted by UK-based business organizations is to reinvest the entire value charged for purchasing the business, and the same will be depreciated over a period.

The advertising agency, Interbrand, has suggested a different method of brand value accounting. This method, as well as the other methods proposed by industry experts, considers the brand's future sales potential as well as its current market share to reach a definitive brand equity or brand power figure.

Therefore, one of the models adopted by the industry accounts in terms of value for the brand's net profit gained over the past three consecutive years. To this is applied a score derived from the calculation of certain primary product-related factors such as brand dominance, market share, trend, loyalty, etc. Some weight age is given to each of the factors, and the total score is then converted to a certain value using a multiple that is again derived from a market study carried out for that sector.

Likewise, there are a variety of other models and approaches suggested by industry experts. Both models use a mix of qualitative and quantitative variables to achieve a tangible brand equity value. Some of the well-known models are the Brand Equity Calculator, Longman Moran, and Leo Burnett's Consumer Brand Equity Brand Asset, Transformation Model Equity Monitor, etc. The considerations included in the above vary from product value to consumer behavior, perception, market share, price group, longevity, etc. A rational framework for calculating brand equity is important not only for the accountants but also for the business organization looking to buy a brand. Assessing a product and setting the right price or premium for the brand requires a validated process and template to guide decision-making. It is also true that one model is unable to satisfy both finance and account staff as well as business managers because the perceptions and purpose of evaluation of each are different. As brands are essential to the organizations ' growth and business strategy, decision-makers would need to be validated, clear models to direct them in making decisions. In addition to the models, they would need to evaluate brand equity from many other product portfolio perspectives, the brand's growth potential to see if a brand was the right choice. If there is a strategic synergy between the product and the business needs of the buyer, then the brand value is likely to shift, and the buyer may find it necessary to pay a premium above and beyond the perceived brand value. It makes sense to buy the product at what cost is a decision that is important to the buyer. In this decision-making process, brand-value templates will certainly help him.

If you're branding ell, you can get your brand name humming. Your reputation is passed on by happy customers and fans of your services, which ensures that by referrals alone, you get a lot more business. When done correctly, branding has a strong snowball effect. How do you start to set up a brand name? Looking at other popular brands in your industry is a great place to start. Follow social media industry leaders and check their website. Who distinguishes them from each other? What's your brand's message? How are you feeling? Look at the many ways they set up their brand and take lessons from us. Many of these methods can be applied when creating the brand name of your own company.

1.6 Brand Equality

During any marketing crisis — whether it's a product recall, employee strike, or any other case of company turmoil— a strong brand establishes emotional relationships with its clients, making people feel positive about a business or service, even the toughest times.

Brand equity is valuable in building the credibility, trust, and market reach of your company. Therefore, it will have a higher value for your products and services. For example, why do consumers prefer Tylenol, the brand name painkiller, over non-branded alternatives that would add value to them? Because the brand is strong, trustworthy, and identifiable. Through strong brand value, they can charge more for the drug and build brand extensions, such as releasing a new product, Tylenol PM.

Apple is an example of a long-term brand equity business. By positioning itself as a creative maverick in the tech industry, it has created an iconic brand. The brand focuses on product quality but also uses separate, innovative marketing to promote both the selling of a specific product and the overall brand. The commercial revealed the product's outstanding features through the distinct prism that is the Apple brand as they launched the MacBook Air laptop.

A smart brand seeks to establish this foundation of trust from the outset, building and nurturing relationships with people, so that when it faces a crisis, the belief system of the consumers will be strong enough to serve as a cornerstone for the business to respond, react and survive.

Disaster lessons Consider, for example, Blue Bell Creameries ' recent product recall, which forced the company to cut into its brand equity.

Despite the massive recall of the product from stores in Texas and Oklahoma, consumers of Blue Bell are eager to support the revival of the brand. Recently, the Houston Chronicle announced that supporters are going so far as to hold prayer vigils in Brenham, Texas, for the brand's positive return. Other consumers, upon their return, announce their intention to purchase three times as much merchandise from the shelves.

Organizations can not foresee a crisis, but what they can do is build a positive brand relationship that serves as a pillar of confidence to avoid the potential dangers that may pose the marketplace.

The following takeaways are crucial to solving a crisis as it relates to brand equity.

1. Communicate directly with your consumers Paul Kruse, CEO of Blue Bell, has yet to discuss the financial impact of the recall on the bottom line of the company. Rather, he has shown genuine concern for the loyal customers of the company and gave his 100% pledge to do all he could to make it right. He spoke to the health of customers and his undying dedication to preserving their trust.

2. Keep your correspondence correct Don't use timeliness as an excuse to withhold information. In other words, when gathering the data, it's all right to say, "We don't know yet." Continue to provide information and progress reports.

3. Be frank Talk honestly to consumers with a desire to make things right, not a defensive tactic to restore shareholder interest and recover financial losses.

4. Include all communication channels as the message is communicated. Always consider and use all communication channels that can act as consumer touchpoints because people are unique in the way they consume media.

The argument is that, by creating lasting emotional relationships with customers, successful brands create more than a logo, they establish a "Trustmark."

4. Brand awareness: Brand perception is what customers think reflects a product or service, not what the brand-owned company thinks it does. The customer owns the image of the brand, not the product.

5. Positive or negative effects: When customers respond positively to a brand, the company's reputation, goods, and bottom line will benefit, while the opposite effect will be a negative customer reaction.

6. Value: Positive effects yield tangible and intangible value—tangible effects include increased profit or revenue; intangible effects are brand awareness and goodwill. Negative effects can minimize both tangible and intangible effects. Uber, for instance, had a positive trend in late 2016. Still, a series of controversies ranging from racism to espionage had a negative impact on his image, bottom line, and brand equity, in addition, consumers tend to remain loyal to those brands based on their established belief system and the brand's feeling. Brand equity of a company is key to successfully managing and overcoming a marketing crisis, then, or the way a brand makes its customers feel.

What happens next after you've successfully branded your company? Protecting your branding efforts is important because your business's reputation depends on it! If you are not diligent in preserving the effectiveness of your branding campaign, your brand image will easily be destroyed. Here are some points to help you take care of the brand you've worked so hard to build: Don't take your brand for granted—

just because your brand image is reputable and recognizable doesn't mean that you can stop investing time and effort in it. In order to stay ahead of competitors and meet their target market, it is essential for business managers to sustain and refresh their brand continuously. Small improvements can lead to a major difference here and there when it comes to branding. Keep a close eye on rivals to see if, in a certain region, you need to step up the branding game.

Stay consistent with your brand image–Consistency in the level of service/products you offer, how you interact with consumers, and other areas are important after you have built up a successful brand. Small branding improvements that are clear upgrades will help consumers, but don't get so inconsistent with your branding that customers think your company is undistinguishable or unreliable.

Talk Thoughtfully–Think about your business ' message before you talk, make a press release, write something for your website, or make a statement otherwise. Words can easily kill the reputation of a brand and can damage your business. Make sure that your words suit your brand's mission and aim to make your brand effective.

Good behavior–Each company employee reflects your business ' character and can benefit or hurt the branding. Being well and representing the business is critical for every employee. Otherwise, because of the bad behavior that scares off customers, your company could experience a drop-in sale.

Practice Good Customer Service–If you have an issue with your service or product, customers should always have a way to reach you. Fast answers are needed to ensure that customers appreciate their service and loyalty to them. Just not answering the question or concern of a customer means you don't value them. The consumer would undoubtedly let others know about the lack of good customer service, and the brand is going to suffer.

Maintain Online Appearance–Many of us have a little too much fun from time to time, but that certainly doesn't mean you have to paste incriminating photos around your social media sites. If you're the face of the company or a famous employee, you'll need to keep your profile online. Do not jeopardize the reputation because consumers can see that you may not always have the best behavior.

No Lies–After successfully branding your business, one of the most important tips to follow is not to lie to your audience. It's almost impossible to recover it once you lose the trust of a customer. It is unethical to lie to customers for any reason, it will let potential customers know about your dishonesty, and you will miss out on a lot of new business. Make sure that your branding and what you say about your business, in general, is honest and that you are truly portraying who you are as a business. By being honest, it's always easier to maintain branding and consumer satisfaction.

Chapter 2: How to make Real Estate Brand Identity

The real estate sector is one of today's most competitive industries. You need to mark yourself to be a good realtor so you can differentiate yourself from your competition. Through Branding, you can do this. In the context of advertising communication resources such as logos, taglines, and other branding devices, Branding uses symbolism to be identified, separated from the competition, and recognizable. You can set yourself apart and build a reputation in many ways.

The internet is such a major part of the home buying process to help you develop your brand is essential to have as an individual realtor or realtor team. Include information about yourself on your website, such as your core values, your background, why you're passionate about real estate, your slogan, and a photo of yourself and/or your team. Think about what your ideas for the price are and what separates you from the other realtors in your field and then translate it to your website. This will allow potential homebuyers to get to know you and have faith in finding their dream home. Also, a website is very important for your brand because that's where most people start looking for a home. The National Association of Realtors shared that the first step in the home buying cycle was to look for properties online for 44 percent of home buyers.

You will be dealing with people from every area and part of real estate as an investor in immovable property from managers of property to residents and agents of real estate. Growing needs a slightly different method of managing, and the brand identity should be sufficiently inclusive to avoid alienating any of them.

In many ways, you are likely to deal with property managers down the line. You'll want to leave a positive impression whenever you do. This will help with a quality brand identity. Real estate agents are a great source of up-to-date data from the industry. They are important connections to have, and when talking about your own brand, this should be considered.

Your USP is your single point of sale. What's different from your rivals, and what's great about how you do things? This is the character that swings on your label. Focus on a specific and ideally execute the particular-don't seek to be all things to all people. If you can end up with a confusing brand identity, and more importantly, you probably won't be able to achieve the high standard and value you're trying to deliver.

This next step in creating a brand identity for your real estate is all about identifying who you stand for. This will probably also include elements of your statement of purpose and core values that are usually defined in your business plan for real estate.

All you do should be done on all platforms and collateral with accuracy. You would also need to constantly keep up with your brand recognition and always remember what you're aiming for. Having a vision and a mission statement will help to give you long-term emphasis and credibility, but as time changes and you're not adamant that you're not going to rebrand the product and whatever happens to your brand, it's more likely than not to grow over time.

"The brand is the sum of the views, ideas, and knowledge of your consumers, as Entrepreneur puts it. It's your business' eyes, personality, and values— and everything in between.

"Your name shines through in customer relationships. And how you interact with your community is reflected in this.

Successful marketing is true to its market of top real estate agents. This gives them the advantage they need over their rivals, making a lasting positive impact in the minds of consumers.

But it doesn't happen overnight for a brand which produces results. The best marketing strategies for real estate come from deliberate, frank insight into specific business and its unique path forward.

That property company has a unique story to tell. Whether they are different services, principles, the management, or the field in which they are trained-no, one is the same. If you tell your story in a way that differentiates your real estate business from your rivals, you introduce yourself to the public. You must first decide who you are as a company and then back it up with a memorable visual brand identity to effectively communicate your message and create a powerful real estate brand.

Prospects already have a strong view of your real estate business before searching for you online or making inquiries–this impression was formed mostly by meeting marketing materials from your business. Therefore, in your marketing, your visual identity plays an important role.

You can paint an optimistic and unforgettable picture of who you are as a real estate brand with a strong and compelling visual identity while building an emotional connection and passing on your core message to your target audience.

What is a Brand Identity Visual?

You need to build a distinguishable personality that carries through all design and marketing elements in order to have a strong real estate business and gain further mandates. Elements like; photo design, fonts, color scheme, logo, tone of writing—all make up your visual identity, which is important for consistently telling the story of your real estate business. Therefore, in any communication strategy, a visual brand identity is important and is the first step in winning both print and online advertising.

Why do you need a strong visual identity for the brand?

Your industry reputation, particularly for first impressions, is not focused on your services alone. Once you create a strong visual identity, which is identifiable, reflects the personality of your real estate brand and identifies you, you will gain many advantages, including Brand Awareness If you develop a strong image for your real estate brand, you can increase the likelihood that more consumers will remember your real estate business and the services you offer—thereby raising brand awareness.

Build Trust Once potential customers know who you are, you are essentially building a relationship with them to make your real estate brand more trustworthy, reliable, and credible.

Cost-Effective There is staying power in a well-designed and thought-out visual identity. The test of time will stand a strong visual identity-saving you from constantly changing and reinventing your logo and other marketing materials.

How to build a brand identity that is unforgettable?

The key to good visual brand identity is to make sure it is well-defined, cantered, unique, impactful, and, most importantly, memorable. There are also other steps you need to take before you start creating your visual identity: study your brand Whether you are developing your visual brand identity from scratch or just refining it, this is the most important step. You're going to lay the groundwork here and learn about your product as much as you can. Analyze everything from which your competitors, target audience, services, and goals are, and accurately determine what your current corporate identity is. All this information can be obtained by interviews with staff, customer surveys, and internal reviews — the more information you can provide to the company that better designs or re-designs your visual identity.

Creating a Design Once all the necessary information has been obtained, you are now able to work with a design agency to come up with visual representations of the message of your product. Find the best way to communicate the personality, priorities, and values of your real estate brand visually-bringing your message to life through visuals and elements of design.

You can start designing when you know what style you're looking for. Choose a design studio that you can work with, then sit back and let them create a logo that will express your message clearly and endorse art. Try to take over the less design process as it may bear a logo you like, but it may not be practical for potential clients.

It is of utmost importance in the highly competitive real estate industry that your business brand has an influential visual language that will consistently echo your message through sound design in every aspect of your marketing efforts.

2.1 Importance of Brand building

It's changing times. In choosing brands to do business with, customers today are more concerned about than just what products or services they offer — they are worried about what kind of different brands are having in the world. And if you're going to take the brand to the next stage, you need a sense of purpose— a sense of purpose that binds your audience.

Your product intent can have a significant impact on how the consumer views your brand— and can eventually be the driving force behind your success.

You may think branding is a suitable method for selling commercial products, but your real estate business will benefit from many of the same benefits. Agents with a consistent and robust name differentiate themselves from the competition. Here are three reasons why property matters for a smart brand identity.

This could be the most apparent advantage of developing a separate brand. Recognition of your name means that you are well-known and well-known. This can be done in a few different ways: an eye-catching icon, a catchy catchphrase, or a unique community undertaking. Seeing and hearing your name listed will cause your logo or slogan with appropriate exposure or effect. And maybe you will be remembered as the person who sells freezes at the street sale in the community and by that credibility will establish a positive association. When someone is planning to buy or selling a home, the agents will stand out in the minds of potential customers.

While it is essential to have a unique and recognizable product, you should also maintain the integrity of your brand. Consider your best clients to write a testimonial for you if you are an experienced real estate professional that can be posted on a website or printed in a brochure. It is even more effective if you can get permission from your client to post a photo of them in their home, putting their faces behind their names. If you're new to the industry, you can still do some things to give credibility to your product. This could be by listing your education, professional affiliations, or knowledge and experience in related areas such as interior design or building.

This one takes a bit more time and effort to develop and is more about the customer's experience interacting with you. Be your word's individual and meet your obligations. If you promise to follow up with the study of market data or the name of a preferred legal service, stick to it. Over time, you will become known for being a reliable and trustworthy professional. Trustworthiness is an even more important feature when it comes to customer referrals to friends and family, and you'll see how being a name people can rely on will benefit you even more.

A label is used to illustrate the company's or business ' main objective. It will clearly make people aware of our company and build an image among the people, so they can easily spot our brand from other related brands. They should be able to recognize our service by looking at the label.

 Customers will only buy a service from a company they trust because, on some distrusted basis, no one will ruin their precious time and money. Branding will help you build trust value in the clients ' hands. When anywhere, in t-shirts, business cards, advertising, etc., our new brand logo and name are shown, people can easily identify us and start to consider us a trusted company.

The ultimate goal of branding, of course, is to attract new people to your market and eventually turn them into your loyal customers. Branding allows the company to build a strong customer network. It will regulate your brand name throughout the world and help make potential customers for your company.

Many real estate agents recognize advertising's value. To order for their business to grow, real estate agents need to communicate with new customers continually, and for this purpose, everything from city billboards to internet advertising needs to be considered.

But while the importance of advertising is indisputable, if you have a clear sense of your brand identity, this advertising will go much further. Branding is a complicated thing for many real estate agents, especially those who have just started. Although figuring out how to get your real estate license in California, for instance, or how to get endorsed by a brokerage is relatively easy, developing a brand identity requires a certain amount of trial and error.

No brands arrive immediately at their final form, and if you're like most realtors, you're probably going to try out some different ideas before you settle down on one that works. But once you do, you will find the work worth the effort: a brand identity is important to long-term success in the real estate industry, and building a connection in the minds of consumers between you as an agent and the type of real estate you are working with will help ensure a steady flow of buyers. Here's just a couple of reasons.

A Brand Identity Makes You Identifiable The most important reason to think carefully about your brand identity is that it makes you more identifiable and, therefore, more likely to attract new clients. For example, if you deal mostly with luxury sales, or rural sales, or specialize in sales in an ethnic group, creating a brand identity around that is a great way to attract the kinds of customers you want.

A Brand Identity Establishes Trustworthiness in a real estate transaction, all real estate agents understand the importance of trust. For most people, owning a house is an important matter, and it's one that will have a definitive impact on their lives for years to come.

Establishing a brand identity and consumer loyalty strengthens your reputation and shows that you know what you are doing and will deliver results to potential customers immediately.

A Brand Identity Helps Create Loyalty It is typical for agents in the housing industry to concentrate more on acquiring new leaders rather than customer retention. Over the course of their lives, the average American travels only about eleven times, and only a few of those movements will include buying a new property, so what are the chances that a realtor will get repeat clients?

The reality is that fostering customer loyalty through brand identity is a key strategy for effective realtors, not only because it can secure future profits down the road, but because brand-loyal customers are more liable to recommend the company to their friends and family. It may take some time to select on the right product, and you may even want to invest in brand experts ' professional help. But if you want to succeed as a real estate agent, it is important to develop a strong brand identity early on.

Next, attention was given to the product definition. It has been pointed out that the product idea is at the heart of an effective business plan for real estate. It was explained that the branding value is difficult to estimate due to its appearance and uniqueness feeling. Differentiation has been argued to achieve its highest level when consideration is given to the strengths and weaknesses of the company and its rivals. Next, consideration was given to the brand development and benefits. In particular, it was reported that there are strong, beneficial, and specific connections in the successful brand model. The first step of the customer-based Brand Equity Model is the execution of analyses that collect awareness of consumers, rivals, products, current, and backup organizations. Secondly, it established product features, target, and content. In general, it has been shown that the brand concept is essentially a combination of many issues and that all brand elements must be exposed to a customer. The brand concept structure solution was then described for the real estate business, and the key features of the implementation process were presented. It has stressed the need to replace traditional leadership with informal leadership. Benchmarking has been used as a method to expose the strengths and weaknesses of the architecture of the product design. Place, products, quality, and identity are identified as the four main components of the brand definition. The position was a rare balance between the position of purpose and activity. Significant functional location concerns were: central or nodal position, connections to traffic, Marketers have access to a treasure of data in the digital age that can be used to direct decision-making. In taking an evidence-based approach to what works and what doesn't, the key factors that drive business success can be established, and our marketing strategies adapted to proof rather than promises.

This may look like a great idea on the ground. And that's it. The abundance of available data, however, has resulted in a large-scale switch to conversion-focused logical marketing deals of a short-term nature, with fewer resources dedicated to long-term success brand building.

"Strategies that produce the greatest short-term revenue results are the opposite of the best long-term growth strategies."-Source in the latest book by Peter Field, "Why aren't we doing this? How long-term brand building drives profitability, "he takes a detailed look at how, to the detriment of long-term brand value, the requirement for short-term results is achieved. The book advocates the importance of taking a balanced approach to advertising and marketing activities by drawing on a vast amount of evidence.

We have successfully implemented a variety of strategic approaches for our consumers through the creation of Hypergiant, a results-driven digital marketing agency, which combines conversion-focused PPC ads and retargeting with a brand-building to make the best of both worlds.

This article explores our experience of juggling short and long-term approaches and how our experiences represent the suggestions made in the latest book by Peter Field.

Tunnel vision versus broad reach "Paid quest is a helpful short-term sales tool but is not successful on its own to work long-term sustained growth; it needs to work alongside the brand building."-Source There is a mistaken belief among many marketers that piling short-term results together will lead to long-term productivity growth. Unfortunately, this profit-centered approach defies the market's realities: for sustained periods, it does not work (on its own).

Through combining conversion-oriented ads with strategic brand-building practices, however, we were able to provide our consumers with both higher profit margins and better ad efficiency. We use a combination of the following steps to maximize product visibility and cognitive availability:

Search engine optimization - To ensure that the products of our customers are the first deals to appear at each point of the customer's purchasing journey.

Content development embodies storytelling concepts in a way that illustrates what separates our consumers ' brands and helps to conquer the rankings of search engines.

Social media management to create an advocacy group and grow a hot audience for conversion-oriented remarketing and custom offers.

Demonstrate social proof by hacking PR and incorporating testimonials at the right moments into product collateral.

We find that our sales-focused efforts are much more successful as a result, beginning with what makes the product unique on the market and executing paid advertising campaigns from this basis.

The plan should always continue. All too often, marketers tend to jump into action without having to take the long-term picture into consideration. Most businesses want to see immediate results, which does not give enough time for their organizations to create cognitive capacity in the minds of potential customers. This usually results in an unbalanced focus on selling and converting existing prospects instead of increasing the audience.

The allure to develop rational' offer-based' advertising at the expense of creative campaigns is very tempting with the granular data available. The problem in this approach is that there is no recognizable brand collateral being created. If consumers can reorder the same item, evidence indicates that they are more likely to buy what's on sale rather than searching for the brand in question.

In the marketing world, there is a common mistake that the larger, the better. People often think that more web traffic means more clients, more followers mean more legitimate opportunities, and more backlinks automatically lead to better rankings of search engines.

Although there is some truth in this notion, and it cannot be understated the importance of reaching new customers, it is important to focus on generating high quality, valid leads. While extending the scope of your marketing activities, make sure that at every step along the way, you target the right people.

2.2 Monitoring Brand Growth

You are facing a tough world of sales and advertising, and fragmented news, marginal pressure, and real estate shelf rivalry are competing for your marketing dollar.

Nevertheless, being a strong brand has never been more important despite the challenges. The war can only be fought on cost without strong branding that catches attention and is recognizable and convincing. Simply put, successful brands are gaining market share and loyalty. We demand higher premiums, as well.

What we measure

To achieve and maintain product growth is to tap into and drive demand and communicate with your consumers through the right deals and the right conversations. In order to win, you need to understand how your brand affects the intention to buy and sell. Through correlating its own measure of brand equity with market share and customer loyalty, Nielsen establishes this correlation.

We're giving you a clear picture of who is doing what and why. We will show you which category attributes most value to your consumers, how your brand compares with competitors, and which tactics will cultivate stronger brand equity to achieve growth in revenue.

How we do it

We know brands better than anyone else, and we're passionate about them. Our methods are being tried and tested, and we have helped brands to succeed in 87 markets around the globe by applying hundreds of categories of learning from thousands of brand studies.

Our methodology has been endorsed in-market to have a significant brand share correlation, and our research work is powered by a large normative database of over 16,000 global brands.

Simply put, Nielsen's brand equity metric is an objective purchasing intent barometer and is directly related to market share. This ensures we can forecast the business impact of achieving these targets as we help you develop strategies and priorities to build your brand.

There are different ways in which businesses can start Brand Monitoring if they don't already do it and increase the value they gain from it substantially if they have already begun doing something.

Off the shelf solutions

These solutions are generic, collecting a limited amount of data and selling it to everyone for a fee. You get the same information that your rival gets (which cannot be customized). The benefit you obtain from such solutions is marginal and will essentially fulfill your desire to have a solution in place but will not give you any competitive advantage.

Off the shelf products mainly deal with text-based data, and the proliferation of cameras in each smartphone, the new content generated, is usually based on video or image.

Many businesses start off the shelf solutions and soon realize that an extremely limited amount of quality can be extracted from such cookie cutter and inflexible solutions.

Custom solutions

A solution designed for you alone, with your preferences and desires in mindfully configurable to your changing needs—that's what we hope.

All of this is usually associated with the high cost and lengthy deadlines, but the aim of the company is to build this solution for you at a very affordable cost and within weeks. While the prices may be higher than the "off the shelf solutions," the relative value for your dollars that you gain will be dramatically and proportionally higher. Time-to-market is much faster than self-constructed solutions because we have a catalog of pre-constructed components that we can quickly assemble to create a personalized solution rather than starting from scratch.

There are clear examples of "Product Tracking" that people immediately associate with negative product comparisons, and "Social Media" is the largest source.

Nonetheless, there are many online sources that have on a daily basis a subtle and perhaps not so obvious effect on a product. Some of these outlets are e-commerce sites such as Amazon or eBay (lower price, higher ratings and competitive product position) Online forums (what's said about your brand) Review sites such as Yelp or TripAdvisor or any other niche sites (what brand people recommend) Self-review areas at sites like Amazon where users can review goods using Video or Image derived.

Web Scraping benefits

In the web, scripting continues to be applied successfully to track and collect online information and present the data in an instantaneous manner to allow company executives to make decisions at a micro or macro level.

If you are an executive of the company and have not considered using such products, you are already slipping behind your rivals. For a while, they have used these methods or recently approached businesses.

Web scraping helps to collect and order unorganized data in ordered and manageable formats. So, if your brand is discussed in multiple ways, like on social media, forums, or comments, you can set the algorithm of scraping tool only to collect data that contains the brand's preference. As a result, marketers and business owners around the brand will gage customer feelings and change their advertising release strategy to increase visibility.

Look around, and you will find numerous methods for web scraping, ranging from manual to fully automated systems. Your web scraper will help create amazing insights from seemingly random bits of data (both in structured and unstructured format) from credibility tracking to website monitoring.

The idea of internet scraping is revolutionizing the business use of big data. Retailers are on cloud nine with its industry-wide availability. Here's how the retail market uses Web Scraping's ability to track products.

Recent e-commerce developments reveal the need for a strong online presence. From this aspect, web scraping takes a cue, scraping comments, and profiles on websites. Web scraping can help you achieve digital brand intelligence and tracking by providing you with a crystal-clear image of product quality, consumer activity, and interactions.

Detection of fraudulent reviews Present-day buyers have this unique habit of referring to reviews before their purchase decisions are finalized. Web scraping helps to identify opinion-spamming so that fake reviews can be found. It will also provide support to track, update, streamline, or block comments depending on your business needs.

Web data mining online reputation management helps to identify methods for achieving the ORM goals. You can learn about both the impactful and vulnerable areas of online reputation management with the aid of the scraped info. The web crawler can classify demographic opinions such as age group, race, emotions, and position of GEO.

Since social media is one of the essential factors for retailers, Scrape Social Media websites and collecting information from Twitter will be crucial. Web scraping software can allow you to look at your social media product along with social media analytics data collection. Through social media channels like Twitter monitoring services, you will strengthen the identity of your company even more than before.

Web scraping for product tracking allows you to look at your company as a general consumer with a second pair of eyes. Considering the flowing customer mood on the market during a business season, you may be able to correct or simply invent better ways to turn the target audience in favor of your product. Future business strategies and brand responses could be designed through a systematic approach to online brand intelligence and monitoring, keeping your business prepared for both types of scenarios.

Organizations collect information from Twitter to help them understand' what's happening' in their business field for successful site scraping. In terms of brand awareness, consumer engagement, and brand recognition, they often come closer to reality in the perceptions of their clientele. Web scraping professionals or businesses scrap social media websites to capture specific brand or competitor-related data that has the potential to impact your business growth. The information is handled and structured to collect important facts and reference building facts. Brand monitoring professionals are planning the potential plan for your brand, considering the facts gathered by site scraping. The data obtained from web scraping helps in—

- Understanding the real product potential.
- Expanding market exposure.
- Developing brand reach.
- Analyzing a brand's range and potential.
- Designing thoughtful and insightful brand strategies

Web scraping offers a company ample base of knowledge that could be used to formulate the future and make possible changes to the current business strategy.

Web scraping advantages
Web scraping made things smooth for companies engaged in brand management and effective brand tracking. There's no doubt that web scraping for brand monitoring comes with huge benefits.

Improved customer insight
When you have knowledge about your consumer base through social media channels, you're in a strong position to

represent your positive image as a brand. You will develop strategies more efficiently with more realistic information on your hands and make realistic goals for the development of your product. Social media analysis also allows advertisers to create highly targeted and personalized marketing messages, leading to a greater probability of conversion of sales.

Monitoring the Competition
Web scraping helps you to find out where your product is in the competitive market. A brand's real presence in the targeted market allows you to get a clear picture of your current business scenario. You may strengthen your brand image by carefully eliminating competition in your market class.

If the product management team keeps track of all social media channels, it's easier for you to keep up-to-date on sites like Facebook, Twitter, and discussion forums, etc. On these internet portals, you might have a deep knowledge of consumer behavior linked to your product and your competitors.

Increased consumer satisfaction and sales
Web scraping credibility monitoring helps to generate expected response in times of crisis. It also mends the communication gap between the consumer and the brand, thus improving the satisfaction of the consumer. It inevitably results in confidence-building and brand loyalty enhancing the sales of your product.

2.2 Brand Identity: Why It Matters in Real estate?

For any organization, brand identity is important as it essentially defines how people perceive what they must give. Before, together with other important product elements, we explained the entire concept in a little more detail. Today, many companies have the label itself, and only then there is a range of branded products. Real estate is special because a brand is a commodity in most situations. And that adds to the value of brand identity. After all, it means that not only will people judge what you are doing, but they will also be given an opportunity to see how you are doing it.

In I like art, from a well-tested viewpoint, we approach real-estate brand identity. We first need to know what your product stands for in order to choose the right brand approach. This means it can't be a profit-making business as its sole purpose. There's a need for a narrative behind it, a feeling. Customers love to spend money when the investment is really appealing to them, not when it's clear that the dealer really wants to get richer at their expense.
Many of the important decisions you make feel unrelated to each other when you manage, market, and promote a company. After all, it does not seem to have much in common to train employees, post on social media, and packing up delivery orders.

However, each of these decisions is the key component of your brand identity.

Why is this important? Brand identity influences two key factors in the growth of your business: brand recognition and brand equity based on customers.

"Your brand identity is how your consumers view you, and ultimately how they feel about you, so both brand awareness and development are incredibly important," Dennery Sanders said.

Together, your brand identity elements should create a coherent picture of your mission and values, reflect the best of your business, and leave a positive impression on your business to customers. This creates awareness among your target market about your brand. You can't expand the market, generate new sales, or build growth opportunities without brand awareness.

The identity of the product is not fixed. In reaction to press coverage, a new product release, or an event on social media, consumer perception of your brand will change rapidly. Companies need to engage in effective brand management and seek to monitor how consumers view their products.

A high self-monitoring brand will quickly engage with customer perceptions, working to change the presentation and perception of their brand when customers do not respond to their current brand identity. On the other hand, a low self-monitoring company will not participate in effective brand management.

Responding to the perception of your product by your consumers is important, Dennery Sanders said: "It is imperative to satisfy your customer base and create a truly persuasive brand identity." This could mean changing your advertising or sales choices if customers do not respond positively.

Though, in response to a negative reaction, you don't want to give up any of your core principles. Low self-monitoring will allow your company to preserve its reputation in the face of changing public opinion when it comes to the communities you want to represent, the ethical values you set, or the message you stand behind.

Long-term, it is important to find a balance between low and high self-monitoring.

So, we're always starting to work on our real-estate projects with a long heart-to-heart meeting with the client, discussing all the ideas about and behind the design, hearing about their unique vision for their company and trying to imagine what we want people to feel like while in the finished building. This helps us focus the whole identity around the emotional appeal expected and creates a bond between the project team and the client. And we know for sure that keeping a positive work environment and friendly relationship makes the whole process of working much more productive and enjoyable for everyone.

Brand identity, otherwise referred to as brand awareness remains a dominant ingredient for long-term success as an investor in real estate. Not only is your company's face and the services you provide a real estate brand identity, but people's overall impression of your business. It also has the power to build trust and customer loyalty while helping to build a reputation as a shareholder. However, a great immovable brand identity has the power to differentiate you from the competition, helping you stake a name for yourself and your company.

The value of creating a clear immovable brand identity is second to none for those new to the industry. Either you are just starting out, or a seasoned vet, the way you are marketing your company, will be the driving force for your future success. That said, the following illustrates why an identity of a real estate brand is critical, the benefits it brings, and how to build one for yourself.

Your immovable brand identity is your companies who, what, when, when, and where. This sets the tone for how your business operates, gives your audience a sense of who you are and what you reflect, and delivers your message and content. Okay, it can turn ordinary consumers into your brand's loyal followers. While it takes time to develop fully, an immovable brand identity can essentially create a visual representation for customers of your product or brand itself.

Often, an image of an immovable product would create a reputation for your brand. The character will be used as part of your online marketing campaign for real estate not only to deliver your message but also to elicit unique feelings in your audience. Essentially, this personality will be used to connect with and exploit the customer base to grow new customers. As an investor, it is not possible to underestimate the power of brand recognition. The following shows the benefits of good branding in real estate: visibility: brand recognition is a prerequisite to success as a small fish in a large pond.
In order to be heard in the competitive real estate marketplace of today, investors will almost always need the branding to get their message across or feel their presence.

The immovable brand identity would help consumers not only create a clear and consistent message that is important to attracting and retaining customers, but also a face to go with it. The mention of the name of your company would carry immediate consumer awareness and confidence, which can have a positive impact on financial results down the line. I should note, however, that while a real estate brand identity is aimed at creating awareness among your peers and future customers, it is largely up to you—the buyer—to see it through. Recall the recognition is not all pleasant.

Trust: A real estate brand identity, together with the ability to produce instant recognition, also has the power to maintain trust. This intangible aspect is a huge benefit for businesses, particularly for real estate investors, as the home of a person is usually an integral part of their livelihood. This is equal to a large amount of emotional commitment, which will hamper a lot of considered untrustworthy real estate investors. The immovable brand identity, however, will help cement a foundation of trust between buyers and sellers, helping to bridge the gap of confidence. That said, for a variety of reasons, brand identity in real estate is important, but none is more important than building consumer trust.

Reputation: reputation is the one thing that every real estate investor lacks when they start first. One of the real estate brand identity's major advantages is the ability to accelerate this process dramatically. As a new investor, your experience level will be at an all-time low relative to your peers, and potential customers will rely on your credibility your company and services. With none to talk about, your brand identity will play a key role not only in developing your reputation but in maintaining and refining it over the years.

A real estate identity is the first step that should be taken by investors starting to build their reputation.

His pledge is the final aspect of a real estate brand identity. As an investor, it is necessary to fulfill that promise— whether to be the fastest or most reliable— every time to obtain the above-mentioned benefits.

Now that we understand the advantages and benefits of having a real estate brand identity, it's time to look at how to create one for a beginner. The following is a five-step guide for building real estate investor brand identity:

Size-Up, The Competition

The first step investors need to do is to evaluate the competition when building a real estate brand identity. Through taking the time to research the local market and analyze what others are doing, investors will gain insight into what the investors ' ideas are focused on and what they are not. Taking the time to size up the market will provide unique opportunities for investors that they didn't know existed when they first started.

Exclusivity is another advantage when assessing the market. Assessing current market brands will help ensure that your marketing is not confused with your competition. For reputation, this is also very critical, as having a copycat approach may result in negative attention.

Define Your Brand

What you stand for is the next step in building your real estate brand identity. In general, this will include elements of your mission statement and core values that are usually defined in your business plan for real estate.

You're going to have to describe it before you can market your product and deliver your message. Investors will ask themselves the following questions to obtain a better understanding of your brand: Who is your target audience? Which group you're trying to reach?

What are the values of your business? Description of the mission?

What are your strengths over your competition? What are you going to provide that others are not going to?

How do you want to view your business with potential customers?

Successful brand development

The successful development of an immovable brand identity is more than just business cards and networking. Once you understand your competition, your brand has been established, and what you represent, now is the time to create it. This will usually include the essential elements such as a logo and a slogan, but will also create an online presence, including a social media network website. This will also include creating your buyer's list; a buyer and sellers' database that might be interested in your services or know somebody that might be.

Deliver Your Brand

The fourth step in creating an immovable brand identity is the implementation stage with a clear message and forum to deliver it. While this will usually include attending a variety of networking events and local real estate meetings, most will include expressing your brand through outlets such as your website, social media, and blog. Therefore, you can also use a direct mail program to bring the product to potential customers.

Refine your brand

Any building wasn't built in a day, nor will the brand identity be established; the key to successful branding strategies will involve continuous improvement. That's not to suggest at some point down the road you're not going to need to rebrand. Your brand will ultimately evolve over time, but you should remain intact with your message and the values you stand for. The way you deliver the message, however, can change over time.

Chapter 3: Creating Real Estate Brand Strategy

Consumers today are market-savvy, and our purchasing decisions are guided by credibility, social evidence, and genuine human connection. We all want to purchase from people we know and trust, so the marketing role of Person-to-Person (P2P) has never been more relevant.

Buyers respect brands that they trust, above all else, and that means providing honesty, expertise, and good communication. While this suggests that brokerages must leverage the personal brands of their agents to win over buyers, it is impossible to ignore the importance of a consistent, brokerage-wide approach.

Without the help that a solid, credible real estate brand gives its realtors, it becomes more difficult to demonstrate honesty and expertise, and it can be a challenge to put in place effective communication practices.

Real estate branding strategies Agencies need to develop a system to create content on a scale and store it in a central hub that everyone can connect to in order to balance the brokerage brand with the personal brand of the realtor.

Consistency is key in marketing, but as the number of channels and media continues to increase, the management of brokerages is becoming increasingly difficult. With designers left battling a flood of requests and rogue agents taking it upon themselves to create content, a brand's value and message can be diluted easily.

Tools they need to create a personal brand without breaching company-wide policies by taking a hands-on approach to producing and distributing top-level product property. The brokerages that do this well recognize that the divisions of branding and marketing need full control when it comes to content creation, but allowing agents the ability to adjust and personalize their content is the way forward.

Marketing managers can control continuity while streamlining workflows by developing templated templates (where a product logo, slogan, colors, and fonts are locked in, but text, images & contact details can be changed).

The aim is not only to build this content central bank but to provide the training as well as the guidance that they need to use it effectively. You will need to think long-term and be flexible in order to make it work. Once a system based on this concept has been introduced by your brokerage, the next step is to look at how content can be used to build and develop a strong brand.

Forward-thinking brokerages know that their virtual environments are much more than brochures online. It's not enough to publish images of assets, though appealing if you're looking to play big.

You will need to look for ways to add value, be insightful, and provide encouragement to step up and move beyond publishing only the planned set of listings.

Improve the website and social channels by putting into practice some of the following suggestions.

• Tell stories that place your target customers in the picture. More than just showing the building or the rooms inside, how can you make your buyers imagine living or working in the house? What about the environment, services, amenities, or community that will have a positive impact on their lifestyles or businesses as a whole?

• Maybe you could interview existing residents or create a story about local restaurants, schools, and shops? There are endless possibilities; you just must tap into the right audience and understand what makes them tick.

• Demonstrate your expertise and provide a head start to your customers. Provide your audience with a reason to trust you by supplying them with answers to their real estate-related questions.

• The aim here is to ensure that you bring true value and not just send out disguised as advice sales messages. Once you produce this type of content, place your customers at the forefront of your mind and try again to get to the heart of who they are and what they want.

• Investing in video and photography, The National Association of Realtors found that 85% of buyers and sellers prefer to work with a video advertising agent, but only 15% of agents currently use video for advertising their listings.

• The embrace of new media is essential for brand survival in today's digital-first landscape, where posts containing video and imagery gain the most traction online.

• Bring your forward-thinking people. In addition to seeking ways to support your agents in creating personal connections, you should also need to find opportunities to have them contribute to the identity of the business.

• Engage the best people with the process of creating content and get them on board. Place them for a Q&A or conversation in front of the audience, then broadcast them live or archive them and use them across your channels.

If you want to create a successful, trustworthy, and engaging brand, remember its sum up: Be motivational, be insightful, add value. Big companies are not the only ones that benefit from improving their brand name. As the Internet is becoming increasingly interactive, it is important that branding is considered by all companies. Your brand name delivers volumes about your unique characteristics, just like your products and services.

Once you've created a brand name effectively, your customers can understand why you're doing what you're doing. It builds trust and reputation, both necessary and fundamental to a branding. Once people know your brand

and trust it, they will be more comfortable doing business with you and will keep buying your products and services repeatedly.

3.1 Targeted Market of real estate

The real estate market is experiencing many ups and downs and is dependent on several factors, such as economic, interest rates, conditions, and job growth.
Regardless of the current behavior of the market, novices and pros can use many strategies that can drive the business forward. These are some of the key strategies that you can use to expand your real estate business and some of the reasons why your company's branding is so important.

1. **Identify the target real estate market**. This is probably the number one strategy you can use as a real estate agent to become truly successful.
Several real estate brokers and companies are focused on a niche market and becoming an industry expert. It gives you a thought of what drives the target market, what risks it entails, and, most importantly, where the short-and long-term demand headed.

For example, an immovable broker who knows the specifics of new local transportation or school project could change his marketing strategies accordingly.
The goal is to increase the media's voice and brand recognition. To calculate the number of business leaders the campaign produces for the real estate sales team, other companies can pick. Plan to measure your success will determine the activities performed during the campaign period, both above and below.

2. **Marketing cost budget** Another important factor in the successful growth of your real estate business is to plan and stick to a marketing budget. If you are planning to launch a new product or service relatively quickly into a large market, then the best strategy would be to go for a network with a large sales force or a large distributor. If you're trying to grow your sales quickly, then you'll have to look through multiple channels at multiple streams of revenue.

There are many ways to spend your dollars on marketing, such as real estate websites, email marketing, social media marketing, and postal marketing.

Your budget must focus on the target audience. For example, consumers in the bay area of San Francisco may need internet-based advertising, whereas customers in a rural area may need a different approach.

You may want to employ an agency to do marketing work for your client, depending on your size and budget. You may have to do this research yourself if you're a smaller or newer product. Even if you can and are willing to pay someone else to do this job on your behalf, you will continue to be highly involved.

3. **Develop a website and using social media** Regardless of the industry, with the help of a professional website, you need to build your presence on the internet and dedicated profiles on social media sites such as Facebook, Twitter, and LinkedIn. These are relatively cheap, with the potential for extensive outreach. You can advertise your business by paying for ad campaigns on search engines such as Google and Bing.

Once your main distribution channels have been identified, you can then outline a summary of the sales plan for each of them. To help you find the best sales tactics to use, use the buyer personas you created above. For example, if your buyer is hanging a lot on Facebook, your sales plan should include sales offers, discounts, coupons, and other marketing tactics on social media.

4. **Encourage referrals, and word-of-mouth** Since the real estate industry is often referred to as a company for individuals, it can be extremely beneficial to build a working relationship with people you meet. You never know when your future business partner will be introduced, or a particularly lucrative offer will be offered. Do what you can, therefore, to build as many partnerships of value as possible. At least, it can lead to referrals to build relationships with like-minded individuals in the same industry.

Although referrals are theoretically another person's efforts to recommend your services, they depend entirely on how you handle yourself in the industry. Make it a priority to provide a nice, one-of-a-kind, and company as it is the foundation for any service based on referrals.

Although simple enough, not many investors are just asking for referrals. It's no shame to let your customers know that your business depends entirely on referrals. You can't get off too hard, though. There is a suitable time to seek referrals. More significantly, perhaps, when you do, show your gratitude. Let them know how helpful they are to you and how grateful you are.

Through referrals from previous customers, the most successful real estate agents create many offers. A potential buyer or seller most appreciates a recommendation from a client.

For example, when referred by a partner, colleague, or relative, new customers are more comfortable choosing a real estate agent. Through giving referral incentives to the individual recruiting a new customer, you can always improve this approach.

5. **Quickly respond to customer queries** We live in a world that moves at a much faster pace than ever before. Responding to customer requests is very critical, or you risk losing new business. You must always have access to email through a smartphone and ensure that you reply as quickly as possible to a customer request. You can't wait in this business until the next day to respond. If you respond promptly, it adds credibility and prestige to your response.

Also, I cannot emphasize the importance of establishing relationships in the industry with individuals. Real estate is a company for individuals. It can only make further efforts in your real estate if you are friends with others. After all, any deal you buy depends entirely on agreeing with you by another party. Why won't it make things easier and work together?

Cross-promoting fellow investors are one of the easiest ways to gain a referral. Promote their products to your customers, and their gratitude will be reciprocated. There are many ways to promote cross-promotion, including a newsletter, on your website, or at an event that you are hosting. Make sure they know that you're going to help them out of your way.

6. **Publish a newsletter on real estate** newsletters, whether print or electronic, can be an effective marketing tool to keep your name in mind with your past and current customers, your sphere of influence, and your prospects. They reinforce your brand, deliver your message, and demonstrate your expertise— all things are done regularly by a successful real estate agent.

If you're serious about your long-term success, then you might consider publishing a weekly or monthly newsletter with updates on current mortgage rates, improvements in real estate regulations, homeownership benefits, how to build a portfolio of real estate investment, local market health checks, etc.

By setting goals for your real estate agent newsletter, you will better determine what type of content you are going to include, what services are going to resonate with your audience, and even what type of model is going to be most successful. All of these variables will contribute to the return on investment of the newsletter, so it's important to set goals. Both current and prospective clients will appreciate such a newsletter's perspectives as it demonstrates your business knowledge and dedication.

7. **Dispel concerns about the need for a real estate agent** Disintermediation refers to the way consumers think about whether they need a real estate agent. Disintermediation advertising seeks to persuade these clients of the quality a real estate professional must bring. You may inform consumers about the need for a real estate agent and attorney during the selling or purchase of a house or piece of land through your website or marketing channels.

You don't need to mention every minor detail of the campaigns you're going to run in a given period at this point— a quarter or the whole year, etc. With a few suggestions and perhaps even a rough suggestion of the budget, you simply need to formulate high-level plans.

8. **Success plan for business** Whether you're a real estate agent or a real estate developer, you're going to need a business plan for real estate development. This is going to set you up for success. With the aid of a business plan for real estate development, you can manage your costs, contingencies, and other risks.

Without such preparations, most people fail when they work in a vacuum. For example, using a well-documented business plan, you can prepare your budget for next year's real estate marketing strategies.

A successful brand strategy starts with a vision of what the product should be portraying or symbolizing. The strategy should also include a mission— a specific attack plan that aims to launch the product.

As with any plan, to review the milestones, periodic reviews should be scheduled. The milestones help the team determine whether the project is on track or whether it is important to change the campaign. The earlier the problems were found and the better addressed. It keeps track of things and guarantees a successful outcome.

9. **Build brand awareness** Like big brand businesses; the real estate business also needs to aim to build its own brand. It might be under the name of your name or the name of

your company. Any technique for real estate sales that you implement will bear in mind this definition.

People also wonder how to sell an immovable property and how to build a business successfully. The response is to plan to build a brand name and use it for years to market the company.

It takes effort and time to establish a successful real estate business. If followed carefully and faithfully, the techniques listed in this article will be worth your effort. Everybody likes a real person on social media. Consumers of social media usually do not purchase talk and corporate pictures into sales. Branding tells people precisely what you're doing and what you're portraying. Your brand name's dream is what remains in the minds of people, not the actual goods and services you sell.

People are responding emotionally to brands. They are doing so much more than with products or advantages. You're building up a name in your industry when your company is strongly advertised. Your image represents you as a key player in your real estate industry, increasing the value in the eyes of your customers automatically. It also means that for your services and products, you can afford to charge more.

3.2 Real Estate Branding Basics

If you're new to the market of this business or if you have a well-known brand, the creation and differentiation of real estate brands are vital steps and essential components of your overall marketing strategy for real estate and home builders. The homebuilder branding specialists work across the globe through domestic and international markets to help define, place, and grow the product narrative, image, and experience for hundreds of homebuilders and new community.

Real estate advertising strategies also need to transcend traditional marketing elements and explicitly encompass all facets of digital marketing to online presence. Most specifically, the product strategy is to remain creative, topical, and engaging with prospective buyers. Real estate branding with experts can help your organization with every aspect of the real estate brand strategy from defining the mission of your company and messaging to designing your logo and creating your tagline. We're ready to step in and help you on your brand journey at any moment.

Uniquely positioned as our core focus with real estate and home builders, we draw on our market information, while also taking the time to listen and understand the business to educate our strategy by helping you create the brand that home buyers seek as their favorite builder repeatedly.

It is a good idea to consider your audience when developing your product. Who are the consumers you want to meet the most? Think about these customers in depth before you determine this; what are their attributes, what motivates them to buy or sell assets, and what is the best way to connect with them? It's an important first step to build your own brand to answer these questions.

Successful realtors understand personal branding's strength. Whether your agent or real estate broker, CEO of Fortune 500 or founder of any company, delivering a persuasive and consistent message resonating with your target audience is more critical than ever. Communicating your personal brand effectively and "why do I choose? "Long-term growth is of paramount importance. Here are some of the tactics that are essential to make this happen.

1. Which makes you remarkable that define your brand?

The initial step is to conduct a self-audit to identify your purpose, strengths, values, and passion. It is important to crystallize your competitive advantage in a fiercely competitive real estate climate. Many real estate practitioners distinguish themselves through their individual achievements (e.g., size of the deal) while others boast added value like JD, MBA, history of the mortgage industry, certification of staging.

Identify terms that best describe your skills to get started: condo expert, software wizard, historic landmark authority, luxury specialist, interior decorator, "clean" specialist. Identify terms that best describe your personality as well: motivated, persistent, truthful. And to get a 360-degree view, understanding how business colleagues and friends interpret you is equally important.

Look at Michele Kleier, president and chairman of Manhattan's leading real estate brokerage firm Kleier Residential, author of the book Hot Property, for a sterling example of a strong personal brand. The brand of Kleier is easy but powerful: "friends, friendships, trust," she says. Together with her, Kleier's husband Ian and daughters

Samantha Kleier-Forbes and Sabrina Kleier-Morgenstern serve as co-stars and co-authors.

"Family is my greatest passion and quality," says Kleier. "The hot family culture we set up at Kleier Residential has helped us to develop our brand in the world's most competitive property market. Our brokers are known as family members and are an important part of success. "

2. Understand your audience

Define your target audience— and provide insight on what pushes them to act. Determine with whom you are speaking: consider age, race, personality, and occupation. Identify the care points of your customers: how can you better address their needs than your competitors? What is your favorite communication channel? It is important to answer each of these questions thoroughly.

3. Know Your Competition

There are more buyers and sellers— and more competition — with increasing confidence in the real estate market. Gather information about who you are up against to stand out. Then, be equal to them. A key question to answer in this process: which niches in your local market are not being exploited? You're ready to put your post in the ground when you find it out.

4. Bring Your Brand to Consistent

It's time to make some noise once you've developed a compelling brand. Clearly infinite stream array: forums, blogs, social media, print collateral, open house signs, advertisements, email advertisement, or a reality TV show.

While most of us will not achieve celebrity status, clear advertising, and visuals that promote the brand, irrespective of the platform, are non-negotiable. Studies have shown that predictable brands are worth around 20% more than inconsistent brands.

Share positive customer testimonials, success stories, content (curated and self-published), professional look, and received media opportunities to build a clear and convincing image. It is not only necessary to view current listings, but also properties that you have successfully closed.

How often are you supposed to share? Focusing on just one social media channel is perfect if time is limited. (To connect to the active site on inactive social media channels, however, is prudent.) And always ensure that you stick to their product standards and policies.

5. Create content that is important (and platform-appropriate)

Great is not enough— to reach the audience, you need to produce outstanding content. Content is more than words, using compelling graphics to get readers interested. So, take a step back, so make sure your post is important to connect before you click the "comment" button. Consider the attitude of the recipient: "What's in it for me? "Whether you're developing articles, blog posts, or videos, make sure the content can be shared, engaged, and actionable. When used properly, irony stimulates more interaction. And don't miss this, "wow! "This is the headline.

6. Professional Community

At the end of the day, buyers and sellers also make decisions based on their relationship with the individual realtor, not the business company. For this reason, engaging in online and offline communities is important. Be transparent: if you receive a negative post or comment, answer it in a timely and professional manner. Your integrity will be respected by prospective and existing customers. Invest in networking as well as regularly joining committees and associations (professional as well as community). Give, and often say, "thank you" before you get.

"It's not about making the deal — it's about the relationship ahead, not selling right now," says Kleier. "If an apartment isn't perfect, we're moving on until we find the right one, no matter how long it takes." Real Estate Mogul and Shark Tank Star Barbara Corcoran are considered to have developed New York City's most successful real estate company — and their success is based on creating and maintaining a trusted brand. "The brand makes the customers trust you before you deserve the trust," says Barbara. "Here's your personal brand to be mastered. And remember: to ensure that your message is heard loud and clear, it needs routine maintenance and monitoring.

7. Defining the brand What makes you outstanding?

The first step is to perform a self-audit to define your intent, abilities, values, and passion. It is important to crystallize your competitive advantage in a fiercely competitive real estate climate. Many real estate practitioners distinguish themselves through their individual achievements (e.g., size of the deal) while others boast added value.

Identify terms that best describe your skills to get started: historic landmark authority, specialist, interior decorator, "clean" specialist. Identify terms that best describe your personality as well: motivated, persistent, truthful. And it is equally important to understand how company colleagues and friends interpret you in order to gain a business deal.

Look to Michele Kleier, founder and chairman of Manhattan's leading real estate brokerage firm Kleier Residential, star of HGTV's Selling New York and writer of book Hot Property, for a sterling example of a strong personal brand. The brand of Kleier is easy but powerful: "friends, relationships, trust," she says. Together with her, Kleier's husband Ian and daughters Samantha Kleier-Forbes and Sabrina Kleier-Morgenstern serve as co-stars and co-authors.

3.3 Essential Points of Real Estate Branding

You need to consider your audience before you even think about building a real estate brand. If you want to make money, the people who are most likely to put a high value on the products you provide should be your audience. It means the people who live in your regional farm area for most real estate professionals. They will be more likely to acknowledge positively to your product and recruit you if you tailor your brand to them. It's that easy.

While at first, this may seem obvious, most managers, groups, and even brokers do not take the time to find out who they are selling to before making branding choices that will have a positive impact on how their company viewed on the market. You need to do as much research as possible on your field area to avoid this error.

You can find a lot of this information from your personal experiences or statement articles, government databases, Wikipedia. Just note that your aim here is to get a general sense of what your target audience might like or hate, so don't get too caught up trying to find accurate numbers.

You'll try to put all this information together to build what marketers call a "buyer profile." A fancy way to answer the question of who your field area would be if they were one person.

You will want to build a "persona" for both buyers and sellers once you have enough details about your field together. While this may feel a bit dumb, it is a crucial step in the branding phase for real estate. Here's why: when you're sitting down to get a great name for your team or company, a slogan or logo, you're going to keep the person you're building in the back of your mind here. If that helps, you can even give them a name! So, if you look at more than ten versions of your logo, you might ask yourself, "what would people think of this logo?"

Here's an example of a buyer you might build if your field area is in San Diego: • Location: Lives or moves to San Diego.

• Age: 30-45

• Combined income: $150,000 + per year

• Home buying experience: first-time homebuyers or out-of-state relocation clients

• Family size: small family

• Common interests: youth soccer, sailing, boating, outdoor activities, cultural activities, antiques, arts and crafts houses in Coronado

• Interested in 3 bedrooms plus home $500,000+

• Political affiliation: Leans Democratic.

Why is a customer going to choose you to help them find a home? Why should a seller pick you for the top dollar to sell their home?

These questions may not be easy to answer if you're a new agent or just started your first team. Nonetheless, don't worry. You are not the first new agent or group to have this problem, and your effective co-workers are positive proof that there are innovative ways to respond to it. Here are major approaches to get you started:

• Are you knowledgeable about tech?

• Do you have a strong ability to market?

• Do you have a great ability to close?

• Do you have a large network of agents, contractors, or lenders?

• How many transactions have you made?

- Are you a small neighborhood specialist?
- How well do you know the surrounding area?
- Are you a Facebook marketing master?
- Have you got a great development eye?
- Do you have a professional background to support your customers?
- How long have you been working in this industry?
- How is the morality of your work?
- Are you an individual-oriented towards data?
- Do you have strong skills in organizing?

Write down all of your strengths and abilities from which you think you can get interested in people in your field area. Try to rank them from the most important, to the least important, once you have a solid list together. You will want to try to integrate the top five or so skills and abilities that you think are most important to your audience while developing your real estate brand.

You need to evaluate the market now that you have a good idea of who your target audience is, and what abilities and strengths you need to give them. The idea is to get a quick overview of your field area's top producing agents, teams, and brokerages. Pay special attention to the name, logo, and slogan of your product.

What's your branding like? Is this more convention? Ultimately, with your name, what can you emulate?

You may want to take screenshots of your websites, save logos, and copy your slogans into a Word document to make the process easier. Having them all together in one location will help you find out what they have in common, or perhaps give you the chance to create a new, unique brand based on your research. For example, are most brands still very traditional in your field area while demographics are changing?

The process of developing a brand and promoting local brand awareness is real estate branding. You usually get a quick glimpse of their logo or name in your mind if you think about the services and products you use daily. Creating brand awareness for your products as a new real estate agent takes time and effort, and for your real estate business, it is a must-do. Your brand represents who you are, what you represent, the quality of service you give, and the value you provide. It's more than just a color scheme or logo. Your credibility is your brand. The purpose of this article is to direct you through the basic steps of personal branding property.

Start by explaining what you're representing. What is your idea of value? Who separates you from other experts in real estate? Write down what you, your target audience, stand for, and why you're different from other agents. Link to your statement of a mission if you wrote one.

Some words and phrases differentiate various brands. Words such as "experienced," "chief," "award-winning," and "specialist" may have a tremendous impact on potential customers, but many use them.

You may not have to fall back on awards and recognition as a new agent. But you may have business experience that can help you negotiate for your customers the best deal. You may be tech-savvy and, for example, expect to sell to the millennial generation.

Hold your target audience in mind when designing your product marketing and choose terms that speak directly to them.

Now what you want to say about yourself creating a sign or emblem that best represents you is the next step in personal property branding. A local designer can translate your vision into a simple symbol telling people who you are and what you can do for them. Some agents decide to leave this move to developers of their website. Others are seeking guidance from students in graphic design or photography. Only ensure that your property logo represents your beliefs and appeals to your target audience. You're also going to understand the balance of your visual identity and how it interacts with your product. It involves using clear fonts, typography, colors, and images.

A word of caution about logos and personal real estate branding: if you work under a broker (as most agents do when they start a real estate career), it is important that you understand the rules and guidelines for the branding of your broker.

For instance: Coldwell Banker, RE / MAX, and other large brokerages have rules to include the broker's logo whenever your property logo is shown. You can find guidelines on logos size (one can't be bigger than the other) and when and where to use them on social media.

Ask your broker for a copy of the advertising policy of the business if in doubt. Display your website broker or advertising collateral to make sure you're on the right track before it has done. It is particularly important if you are a new real estate agent and may not fully comprehend the guidelines.

These few tactics you can use to become a widely recognized brand of real estate. The point of personal branding property is to be innovative, to be original, but most of all, to be on-the-spot. The relation between your logo and your product should be easily visible to prospects. And the more they see it, the more likely they will consider you when they think about real estate the next time.

Branding your immovable is no different from branding in any other industry, except. To decide if your immovable branding is lost in the crowd or looks like a giant among pygmies, are several key aspects.

Here's why: many people perceive almost all real estate companies the same as any other real estate business. The average house buyer could hardly care less if hiring Agent, A, or Agent B and will often make the decision about some seemingly insignificant encounters. In much the same way, the average landlord hires a property manager.

If that's not old news, please repeat it. For the sake of the survival of your venture, note that almost all real estate businesses are treated the same by most customers.

You need to label your company expertly across all your marketing and sales messages to stand out from the crowd. Here are some techniques for how to do that you may want to keep in mind: Branding a company goes beyond logos and letterheads—at root, building a strong brand depends on your ability to add unique value to the lives of your consumers (and make sure they know it).

Author Napoleon Hill puts it well: "People buy your personality and ideas long before they buy your products and services." If you want to have some chance of standing out, your personality and ideas need to offer something special. not "just another agent" or "just another property management business." It is important to understand the needs and expectations of your own unique and specific target group of customers and prospects that you can support the most to grow a successful brand.

Once you know your audience (based on what unique value you can bring to the table that none of your competitors can beat), there is the branding of your real estate company to communicate this understanding across all marketing and sales materials.

Now, the logos and letterheads. When it comes to representing your company, esthetics go a long way. Sometimes, the first thing a prospective customer sees before they even meet you is your ad, direct mail, or website.

Communicating "who you are" as a real estate professional through well-designed product elements such as a logo, website, displays, marketing materials, and advertising campaigns is a vital way to make your first impression (and any subsequent one) positive and enduring.

Childish fonts (I'm watching you, comic sans) and badly rendered graphics convey a disorganized, outdated feeling behind the times. If your homepage, MLS, or classified ads have poorly drawn property images, or if your advertising does not fit across media, potential customers will note. Think of who you'd do business with and what would look like their logos and business materials.

Successful real estate professionals know that in an increasingly competitive market, reliability and integrity build a solid reputation. Sticking to a higher standard is one of the best ways to stay above the noise.

Keeping your Unique Selling Points consistent, you can carve yourself a niche over time and ensure the longevity of your product. Very few real estate companies made it over the past five years, much less than ten. If you can provide consistently unique value and do business with honesty and authenticity, the brand will attract customers who know a good deal when they see it (and who are willing to pay)!

Everyone hears the statement that networking is so essential to building a successful real estate business. You don't know that. It's who you do.

But, beyond just forging new partnerships and getting your name out there, if you have a clearly defined, exclusive, and easily expressed brand, your networking will be most effective. Networking then means simply spreading your Unique Selling Points, telling people what makes you unique (and valuable) in what you do! Make sure you still have plenty of business cards and brochures on your current projects (and ensure your consistent branding included across all media!). The preparation is impressive.

Your real estate brand is at the heart of all the marketing and advertising you'll ever be doing, building on yourself, speeding up your business, creating an identity worthy of the attention of your customers as you aspire for their business. Take your time and never stop building the image of your company, because your business is going to live or die.

Rarely has anything to do with branding yourself in real estate with what the untrained businessman would think. If for nothing else, the branding of real estate has less to do with the outward appearance of your actual company and more to do with how people perceive the owner behind the curtain. And while you can't ignore the effect of the marketing activities of your real estate company, it's not nearly as important as how you represent yourself. That said, conducting yourself in a manner that is conducive to attracting business is in your best interest (and your company's interest). And for what it's worth, there's one way I've seen the world's shareholders achieve tremendous success in their branding efforts: branding themselves at a local level in real estate.

Branding in real estate is about as critical as being able to make a pass. Nonetheless, it is even more critical to be branded locally. After all, if not for local real-estate deal facilitators, what are most real-estate investors? There are exceptions, of course, and many buyers are branching out of their local neighborhoods to finance over long distances, but residential redevelopers are overwhelmingly local. Most of the transactions done by most of today's shareholders take place within the safe boundaries of their own "backyard." Locally investing offers you an edge over anyone looking in on the outside. Investing in your local market will align with a familiarity, one that enhances your neighborhood awareness, improves your reputation, and strengthens your relationships. There's not much more to ask for or even hope for, as an investor.

There's no question about it: it can very quickly tip the scales in your favor to invest locally. There's no reason why a local investor shouldn't have an advantage over those who don't know the area. Nonetheless, it's worth noting that investors don't just get the advantages I've commented on up to this point; they have to fight for them. And there's no better way to become a big investor in your local market than from a local perspective to brand yourself in real estate.

Putting a local spin on your branding efforts on your property can create an instant connection between you and the community. But what does this mean for investors in real estate? Let's look at it.

You need to be smart enough as a real estate investor to ask yourself at least one branding question about what is personal branding? Even a simple understanding of how personal branding is important to contribute to your success as an investor will go a long way, but we don't want to stop there. You will only be able to master your craft and achieve the success you have always dreamed of by a true understanding of the influence personal branding has over the industry in a local market. So, let's begin with the fundamentals.

You've just dreamed of success. So, let's begin with the fundamentals.

Very literally, it sounds exactly like branding yourself in real estate; it's the process of promoting your ideas in a way that advances your career and develops your business. More precisely, the concept of personal branding focuses on the idea of creating a recognizable identity within the culture that you want to represent. There is no reason, with the right strategy, that the person you are building should not be able to establish and maintain beneficial relationships with powerful allies, find more deals, connect with more leads, build trust and loyalty, and even increase your bottom line.

Personal branding in a local community will act as one of your most valuable assets; it is the one thing that will set the tone for your entire career. Note, as a shareholder, your name has a lot of weight, so make sure your name tells you what you want it to be. You'd be wise not to underestimate the power that can carry a single name.

As Tim Ferriss so eloquently puts it, "In a world of misinformation, propaganda, and semi-permanent Google records, personal branding is about controlling your identity— even if you don't own a company. Do you go on a date? Chances are you have Googled your name on your "blank" date. Are you going to an interview with the job? Ditto. "The more you can do to increase your brand name's positive perception, the better it will be. Yet, specifically, how can you do that at a local level.

Luckily, branding yourself in real estate will not be the backbreaking effort others produce. Besides, if you follow the right steps, it can be relatively simple to brand yourself at the local level. Simply identify your audience to get started. Until embarking on any other marketing journeys, be sure to recognize who you want to represent — beyond the shadow of a doubt. Who are you trying to reach, exactly? Who are the best customers for you? What can you solve problems for them? Most specifically, perhaps, how can you build relationships with said customers?

As an investor in real estate, you must first decide what you are hoping to achieve — looking for properties on the wholesale? Does your business plan focus on rehabs? Maybe you are in favor of buying and holding long-term prospects. Whatever the case may be, figure out what you want to do so that the target client can narrow down. Only if you get to know your audience will you be able to put yourself before them.

In doing so, you can build a personal brand that not only makes you look good in the eyes of those you want to impress, but also helps you to navigate what can sometimes be a tricky industry.

I suggest finding something about your own company once you have identified the people you want to communicate with. In other words, what distinguishes you from the contest? What do you have, and not the competition? You will contribute greatly to the development of your brand by answering these simple questions. And to do so, I recommend answering the following questions: • Why would someone choose to partner with you over someone else in your local market?

• What are you going to bring to the table?

• What's the most enthusiastic about you?

• Is there a specific niche that you would fit best?

• Why did you initially start investing in real estate?

By reflecting on what separates you from the competition, you will have a better idea of how to look at the local level to differentiate yourself in real estate. After all, you can even start to entertain a sound marketing plan by understanding both yourself and your audience.

If you know what your company is and who it wants to represent, start the fun part of creating a persona. Remember, you're not selling, you're selling your land. Most importantly, for who you are, people like you, and then what you can do for them — not the other way around. If nothing else, no one will want to work with you if you can't develop any kind of relationship— not even if you're the best in the business. You need to create a connection, one that can make a deal easier.

I maintain that the best investors in real estate are those who can brand themselves locally. That means communicating on more than one level with the group in a given area. To support yourself, consider teaming up with a local company. Better still, start a charity in your area to help those around you. You would be shocked to see how far goodwill in today's market will take a real estate investor. With the advent of the internet, word of mouth can spread incredibly quickly, so it's more important than ever to get off well at a local level.

It's more important than ever to mark yourself in real estate. For belief, otherwise, there is just too much rivalry. That said, branding needs to go beyond the logo design and company coordination's physical aspects. Yes, it's more important for you to prioritize your branding over your company. Only then can you create a person with whom people want to work. And what's a decent real estate investor if people don't want to partner with someone.

Chapter 4: Marketing and Brand development

Brand creation and promotion is the process of creating and improving your brand of professional services. We split the process into three steps as we help companies grow their brands.

• The first move is to match your product plan with your business goals.

• Secondly, all the resources you need to connect with your brands, such as your logo, tagline, and website, are created.

• Eventually, the newly developed or revamped product will be improved.

Your plan for product growth is how you do these activities. We split the product development strategy into ten steps to make the process a little easier.

A good, well-defined brand can make it much easier for your company to grow. But what kind of business do you want? Are you doing organic growth? The reason for your product development strategy is your overall business strategy, so that's the place to start. If you know where you're going to take your business, your brand will help you get there.

Who are your target customers? You make a very big mistake if you say "everybody." Our research shows clearly that high-growth, high-profit companies concentrate on clearly defined target customers — the more focused the concentration, the faster the growth. The more multicultural the target audience will be, the more skewed will be the advertising efforts. So how do you know if you picked the right target group for the client? That's where the next move is coming in.

Organizations conducting comprehensive research on their target customer groups are growing faster and more competitive. Those who do research more often (at least once a quarter) are also growing faster.

Research helps you understand the context and expectations of your target audience, predict their needs, and translate your message into the language that resonates with them. It also tells you how you see the strengths of your company and your current brand. As such, the advertising risk associated with product growth dramatically reduced.

You are now ready to determine the brand positioning of your company in the marketplace of professional services (also known as market positioning). How is your business different from others, and why should potential customers choose to partner with you within your target audience?

A positioning statement is usually 3-5 sentences long and captures the essence of the positioning of your product. In truth, it must be grounded, as you must deliver on what you pledge. It also has to be a bit ambitious, so you have to aspire for something.

Your next move is a marketing plan that converts the positioning of your brand into messages for your target audiences. Usually, the target audiences include potential customers, potential employees, information sources or other influencers, and potential collaboration opportunities, to name a few of the usual suspects.

Although the core product branding will be the same for all markets, different aspects of it will be of interest to each audience. Each audience's messages should illustrate the most relevant points. That audience will also have specific concerns that need to answered, and different types of evidence will be needed to support the messages. All of these needs should address in your messaging strategy. It is an essential step towards making your product meaningful to your target audience.

There is no need for a name change for many companies. But if you're a new company, experience a merger or burdened with a name that doesn't suit your positioning anymore. A name change may be in order. Even if you don't change your company name, it may make sense to better support your product branding with a new logo and tagline. Note, it is not your brand that is your name, logo, and tagline. These are ways to communicate with your brand or to symbolize it. To make it real, you must live it.

And don't make the mistake of publicly revealing the new logo to get a consensus. You don't have the title, logo, and tagline. We are for the business, and they should judge on how well they interact, not how much investors like them. This move could have called "developing the marketing strategy," but we didn't. Alternatively, we are calling for a marketing strategy for content.

What's the reason? In the Internet age, content marketing is particularly suitable for professional services firms. It does all the traditional marketing things, but it does it more efficiently. To attract, cultivate, and prepare candidates, it uses useful educational content.

Note that credibility and exposure drive your product strength. Increasing visibility alone is rarely successful without reinforcing your reputation. That's why traditional advertising or sponsorships that create recognition so often produce misleading results. On the other hand, content marketing also improves exposure and credibility. It's also the best way of making your product important to your target audience — a closed case.

Your website is the most important development resource for your product. It's the place where everyone turns to learn what you're doing, how you're doing it, and who your clients are. It is not possible that prospective customers will choose your company based solely on your website. But if your page sends the wrong message, they might well rule you out.

For a fact, your user content will be home to your website. The content will be the focus of your search engine optimization (SEO) efforts to find you and learn about your business with customers, potential employees, and reference sources. Digital content is essential to any modern strategy for product growth.

These days, there are two types of directories for professional services. The first is a website for advertising. Such a website tells your story and tells you who you are, who you are serving, and what you are doing. In short, it will express your message about your brand. The other type does the latter, generating and cultivating potential new customers as well. We call these websites of high performance.

4.1 How to strengthen brand position in the market

If your target audience not identified correctly, your brand marketing efforts may be unsuccessful. Much more than understanding basic statistics is a target market. Most advertisers are falling into the trap of thinking, "I'm going to target anyone who wants to buy my brand," or I'm going to target all UK peoples. Instead, psychographics can break down a target market and clarify it by creating buying people. You should also have multiple people in this one target market. Such as people with various social media addiction or brand-friendly thoughts. Once a strong target audience has established, move on to a consistent brand.

Educate Employees & Provide Guidelines to achieve a strong and consistent brand identity, you must ensure that your employee advocates are all on a similar page. Firstly, asking the staff to create content can be a daunting idea, as it involves mixing writing skills with an extreme understanding of your brand identity and the messages you want to deliver.

If you are looking for your staff to diversify the content you publish online in marketing campaigns, it may be beneficial to hold training sessions, study groups, and workshops where you can show them how to successfully use your brand identity on various social media platforms and forums. Thanks to a changing market climate, the rules surrounding branding are evolving faster than ever. Millennials ' growth, social media, and thought leadership are driving marketers to think differently and connect in new ways with their customers.

In a world where 64% of consumers have shared-value-based relationships with brands, marketers need to define marketing approaches designed to stop and pay attention to people. If you want to succeed simply, then you need to know how to build a product that becomes the best friend of your customer.

Branding strategies are the plans that organizations use to distinguish from their competitors their products, services, and identities.

Essentially, the long-term brand is a marketing strategy that helps identify what kind of identity you want your consumers to create. It means thinking about what kind of feelings and perceptions you want to connect your audience with your company.

Would you like to be authoritative? Are you sophisticated? Funny? Professional?

A brand is a culmination of all abstract feelings and thoughts that accumulate when thinking about your business in the mind of a customer. Brand strategies are your way of changing those expectations before they meet the goals of your business.

A good brand could lead to better customer loyalty, improved company image, and a more connected identity, according to experts.

As more consumers tend to distinguish between companies with emotion and experience, a brand could be the first step to advance the competitiveness instead of price points and product features. The question is to know how to create an audience-speaking brand?

Once you decide to invest in social media marketing and professional product consulting, note that the following features included in a successful brand.

It is easy to assume that the intent of your brand is a simple thing, like a desire to make money or be popular. The best companies, however, have a drive that goes beyond these apparent elements and distinguishes them from their rivals.

If you can describe why your investors are getting up and going to work every morning, then you can start to develop product strategies that align with your company's fundamental goals and "vision." Although making money is always vital to any company, consumers feel stronger connections to companies that want to do more than a fat paycheck.

Once you have decided what moves your brand forward, you must faithfully adhere to those underlying ideas and provide a clear, recognizable identity for your customers. After all, companies that regularly introduce themselves are up to 4x more likely to experience exposure of the brand, according to studies.

It's easier to achieve reliability than you might think. It simply means analyzing everything you do and asking if it matches in with the picture you present to the world. For example, if you choose to represent a professional and sophisticated persona, you may not want to post a comic on your Facebook wall.

A perfect way to improve the chances of being successful is to build a few "product guidelines." Walmart is a company that has done it extremely well—offering guidance from the editorial voice of the brand to how to use its digital logo.

Note that your brand image quality is also important to your internal communications strategy, as it can help strengthen your core messages and vision with your employees.

Ultimately, while your customers are a significant factor in helping your company succeed, there is another group of people in the business space that often ignored, and that's your staff. If you invest in a new kind of social media marketing or build a brand from scratch, you need your customers ' feedback and buy-in to succeed.

Integrating a brand advocacy strategy into your marketing strategies will help you create a more powerful image. After all, if an organization is being told by multiple people the same things, they are far more reliable than just one person. However, when exchanged by staff, the marketing messages touch up to 561 million more people.

Employee activism reinforces the culture and values of the business that you write about in your press releases and reveals how ideas can be converted into concrete actions and campaigns through your website "about" section.

Share the Right Assets & Tools Employee advocates can create personal, informative content for your company—ideal for long-standing customer relationships. Although providing educational advice is a great way to get started while improving your marketing strategy, you may also need to include practical resources and tools to help employees quickly create and distribute emotional content.

For example, if you want your advocates to share your content, but you know they may have trouble writing it on their own, you can always use a tool like Bamboo to share curated content for your staff on a connected platform. In this way, the workers will simply share relevant content from a list of creations available, rather than writing anything themselves.

Also note that if you ask your staff to share their thoughts on a new product or service, you can help them compose their messages with their voice, so it doesn't sound like an obvious commercial.

For example, some company has an on-board program for workers that involves "discovery courses" for new products, allowing employees to gain a better understanding of the products and services they are speaking about. It helps to make every message sound more natural.

Motivate & Reward Your Advocates Eventually, while many of your employees will be happy to talk about your business and engage in attempts to market social media on your behalf, some will want to know what's in it for them.

Brand ambassadors want to reward for the hard work they do for your business, just like any other employee— the good news is that praising your supporters doesn't have to mean giving them a huge bump in their paycheck. Boss shootings in a group newsletter or small gatherings can be enough to reassure the staff that their time is worth an advocacy strategy.

You may even consider driving some healthy competition among your product advocacy group leaders by posting a monthly leader board highlighting who gets the most social media shares and comments.

Working with people who love social media first is a good way to start adding advocacy to your branding strategies, as these people can help motivate other employees. For example, General Electric used an activism pilot that started to create an army of social sharers, with 500 workers already active on social media.

Branding tactics are all about creating an identity for your company, and who better reveals the unique features of your business, then the people who work in it every day?

If you can inspire your employees to campaign on your behalf, you can also create a brand that is trustworthy, compassionate, purposeful, and more credible! All you required to do is to make sure that the right resources are available to your team.

4.2 Marketing of real estate business

Have you ever noticed how many of your customers saw your billboard on the road that opposes to the number of people on your site?

Digital real estate marketing has given you the ability to monitor the progress of any project you run. It provides complete information such as who viewed your site, several clicks, click on the button call to action, and much more. It gives you the option to make a choice to choose different channels and ad formats that can bring different ideas into your mind to reach your audience more engagingly.

For online real estate advertising, even by building profiles on social media sites, uploading a piece of valuable information, and connecting with your target audience, you can advertise for free.

Consumer brands have been able to attract customers for a long time by creating a whole lifestyle about their brand images, messages, and experiences that recommend a common point of view, a common set of beliefs, membership of a tribe. The same applies to brands of hospitality. Just consider the letter W and not just consider an elegant spring, but you can also guess what kind of music is going to be playing in the lobby, what things are going to be in the mini bar, even how other guests are going to be dressed. That's marketing energy. Brands are more than just a product or ad; the logo is just a shorthand symbol for a whole series of physical, verbal, and emotional attributes and experiences.

The idea of creating a brand to express a lifestyle is a common part of the high-end residential property sales strategy. Still, the strategies are also useful in advertising commercial office properties. A tower is more than square feet, improvements to utilities, and banks on the elevator. It is a special location where a select group of tenants can be drawn. That's why we encourage developers to think about what kind of tenants they want to draw and create a narrative that resonates with that kind of tenant. You need to lead with a different and memorable "hook" to be able to distinguish between otherwise similar properties. What's it like to work there?

The story may focus on the neighborhood's creative energy or the potential mix of tenant types that create a dynamic environment and an opportunity for unexpected encounters. It is also essential in design and architecture, but you need to understand why. It will create distinction by establishing a distinctive point of view that differentiates the property and presenting it in a memorable visual style.

The problem, of course, is to get people to understand what's not yet there for new construction. For 55 Hudson Yards, a building constructed with professional services firms in mind, the brand we created had to feel strong enough to stand up for something that is not built. The story here is about the balance offered by Hudson Yards ' neighboring retail & cultural attractions and the High Line's urban-outdoor experience, coupled with a workplace tailored to an occupant. The sleek, streamlined look— the architectural equivalent of a pinstripe suit — is influenced by the architecture of the house, reflecting the influence of Art Deco and details from early Soho buildings. Choosing a legal format for the brochure, rather than typical letter-size, is a subtle nod to the potential client of the law firm.

Older buildings face another threat. We may still suffer from a perception problem even if they have been upgraded to current infrastructure requirements and refurbished inside and outside, a Chinese development company with a global reach that is embarking on a notable renovation of the entire property, recently purchased the tower.

Although the building hasn't changed since its completion in 1961, the area around it has completely transformed: what used to be the exclusive domain of big banks and white-shoe law firms is now home to businesses ranging from tech start-ups to media giants. Thus, the property is re-imagined as an art square: playing the famous installations of world-renowned artists Isamu Noguchi and Jean Dubuffet and transforming past banking halls and street-level architectural vacuums into restaurants and shops that will enrich the whole area.

We introduced a new name to reflect the transformation: 28 Liberty. This is a comment about its location in Lower Manhattan, not just a street address. And the name establishes an aspirational link to the iconic New York City symbol by evoking the Statue of Liberty that is visible in the distance. (Even the number 28 was carefully chosen: it symbolizes "double wealth" in Chinese.) Identification acts as a "monogram," referring to the visual language of art installations— also used as graphic patterns. Inspired by the famous statue in the harbor, the green color looks nostalgic and fitting for the building's age, but at the same time, new.

No detail is too minimal when it comes to product development — color, design, font, illustration, use of software, even the reception guest experience — as long as it is done in a thoughtful manner and support of a larger idea. Brands articulating a lifestyle are all around us these days. Why shouldn't you also represent a lifestyle choice in the building you work in?

A clear, efficient, and coherent brand strategy and layout helps to communicate the reliability, reputation, value, and experience of your product, regardless of your business size, sector, or venue. Those with a strong brand have a huge competitive advantage when it comes to selling your products and services.

As a realtor, in the last ten years, you may have experienced a major shift. Customers start buying houses differently, mostly beginning with online market analysis and a clear vision of just what they want from their future home.

Digital marketing has been at the forefront of its marketing efforts for best-in-class realtors. From generating new leads to successful sales, digital marketing is now dependent on the real estate industry.

Social media was one of the first changes in the game for realtors looking for ways online to get heard. From buying Facebook Business Ads to sharing new listings photo albums, different social media platforms enabled real estate professionals to create a brand and a prominent business.

For 84 percent of real estate professionals using social media platforms, how can current real estate brokers and real estate practitioners in the United States further distinguish in a saturated market? You can have a much greater impact on your digital marketing campaign than traditional marketing strategies.

Use the following tips to get the results you're looking for to jump-start your digital marketing plan for real estate: An email nurturing campaign is a valuable tool to communicate with new leads and stay relevant to past customers. Ideally, by predetermined actions based on their user profile and prior agreements to you, a well-rounded strategy will funnel potential customers.

According to Smart Insights, with a click-through rate (CTR) of 3%, the average open rate of emails for real estate companies is about 27%. The more relevant content for any customer, the more likely they are interested in opening the email to see what services you are offering.

As a realtor, in the last ten years, you may have experienced a major shift. Customers start buying houses differently, often starting with online market research and a clear vision of exactly what they want from their future home.

Digital marketing has been at the forefront of its marketing efforts for best-in-class realtors. The real estate industry now relies on digital marketing from generating new leads to completing successful transactions.

Real Estate and Digital Marketing Social Media Importance was one of the first changes in the game for realtors looking for ways to be recognized online. From buying Facebook Business Advertising to sharing new listings photo albums, different social media channels allowed real estate business professionals to build a brand and a prominent business.

For 84 percent of real estate professionals using social media platforms, how can current real estate brokers and real estate practitioners in the United States further distinguish in a saturated market? You can have a much greater impact on your digital marketing campaign than traditional marketing strategies.

Use the following techniques to get the results you are looking for to jump-start your digital marketing plan for real estate:

1. Build an Email Campaign: An email nurturing campaign is a valuable tool to communicate with new leaders and stay relevant to past customers regardless of industry. Ideally, by predetermined actions based on their user profile and prior agreements to you, a well-rounded strategy will funnel potential customers.

Working for a plan for cost-effective growth in your sector cost-effectively? $55 is in exchange for every $1 spent on email marketing. By sending custom newsletters, our professional email marketers help your business stay up-to-date with your prospects and existing customers. Check the email marketing opt-in today!

2. Create a user-friendly website: How many times did you open a website just to close it because it wouldn't load fast enough? Realtor websites can sometimes be the nightmare of a web developer with so many images and ties. Nevertheless, real estate professionals may create a responsive website that is designed for mobile browsing with the help of a professional and experienced web designer and a knowledge of what your customers are looking for.

Nearly half of all web browsing done on a mobile device, so if your website not developed accurately, your customers won't be able to visit your page easily. In order to give your customers, the best experience, a mobile-friendly website should include the following content, a list of all new listings content to guide them throughout the home buying process, links to relevant services such as lawyers, movers, and home inspectors. Consider developing and maintain a live chat feature on your website. Your real estate business is extremely people-centered, which means that when you must ask questions, it's important to be available. Investing in live chat technology allows people to connect 24/7 and schedule appointments without speaking to you directly.

3% Primarily use the website of your company to find and engage with you. As if that's not enough, the design of a website was cited by 48 percent of people as the number one factor in determining a business's credibility. What do you say about your company on your website?

3 Pay-Per-Click Advertising: Pay-Per-Click —also known as PPC—advertising is a great strategy for realtors seeking to generate new leads based on ads they pay for each time the ad clicked.

PPC is a great digital marketing possibility for real estate professionals looking for potential customers who might be genuinely interested in their offering, as they only pay when someone clicks through their ad.

PPC advertising can often be targeted at people who have searched in Google or another search engine for linked keywords.

97% of online experiences start with a search engine, but 41% go to the top three paid ads on the search results page. Pay per click is an amazing way to drive to your website more (qualified) visitors and get more leads and sales — FAST! What's the best part? There's no time to wait.

4. Publish blog content: Responsive blog blogs often have 434 million more indexed articles, allowing real estate professionals to achieve better SEO.

A blog is a fantastic way to upgrade your SEO, build a positive online reputation, and provide actionable advice to your customers on buying or selling a home or property. The digital marketing strategy of a real estate company, whether posted on your website or social media, is nothing without valuable content.

Beyond your sensitive website, make sure you write content that buyers and sellers will come back to for answers to their most important real estate questions regularly.

5. Host Virtual Tours: In a good digital marketing campaign, virtual home tours are amazing pieces of content. Such tours not only share video content–which generates revenue for advertisers 49 times faster than non-video users –but a potential customer can get an idea of what a home must give them.

It can be difficult to buy a home, and as an expert in real estate, your job is to make the trip home buying as easy as possible for your customers. Andrew J Carr a famous business person shared some of the more critical qualities that realtors should try to include in successful virtual tours such like using real home footage compared to digital illustrations Ensuring that the tour's video is interactive and responsive across all viewing methods (mobile and desktop) Making the 3D virtual tour user-friendly

6. Creating a Social Media Marketing Strategy: Posting real estate content on your Facebook account is one thing now and then, but a complete social media marketing strategy is what yields the results you're looking for. Some suggestions of useful content to share on your social media channels include: new or existing Group profiles listings (if you're operating a real estate brokerage) Case studies Relevant blog posts Success Stories If you're skilled in digital marketing, you and realize how hard it can be to create a social media strategy and regularly post across all channels. Tools such as Buffer, however, are designed to help make the creation and scheduling of social media content easy and transparent. To develop a social media policy for any real estate business, the most important rule of thumb is to share varied content. Although sharing listings are an important factor in your digital strategy, you want to make sure your content is useful to a wide audience, not just leading to a new home on the internet.

7. Host a Webinar or public meeting: Sharing all of your real estate professionals ' expertise is vital to successful digital marketing. Luckily, strategies like webinars and virtual seminars make it easy to reach a wide audience and remain relevant to the industry. Got Webinar is a webinar hosting platform designed to make it easy to create and host webinar events, and from both ends of the process, it is incredibly user-friendly. For real estate professionals, digital marketing relies heavily on creating inbound leads, so having your name and experience out is key to a productive digital marketing project.

8. Spend Time on SEO: SEO is a vital driving strategy that contributes to your blog or search engine optimization. If done correctly, during specific searches, the website and web pages will appear higher on the results pages of the search engine (SERPs).

Google and other search engines, however, are constantly changing their algorithms, so working more than once on your SEO is important. Keywords are a fundamental aspect of SEO that can make a major difference. Make sure that you include keywords in your SEO strategy in your blog content and website, including high-ranking keywords such as your location and your industry. There are other elements of a successful SEO strategy, including Backlinks Meta titles and descriptions Social media pages Web Directories Because content is such an asset to a good SEO strategy, makes Usually, Google's highest-ranking material is between 1,140 words and 1,285 words, so writing high-value, long-form content regularly may be a good idea.

Begin where 93% of online experiences begin — with search engines. Grow your long-term authority and use search engine optimization (SEO) to get more professional website traffic, leads, and sales.

4.3 Marketing Practises of real estate

Are many people tired of hearing about how good their last social media campaign was when you sell flat? Does it seem like the more time you spend sending out social marketing messages, the less consideration your past and future real estate customers receive?

You're not alone; according to the 2015 Hub Spot Social Media Benchmarks Survey, most real estate agents and brokers have a hard time communicating with consumers via social media.

Time to do a review of social media marketing! If your social media marketing strategies don't get the notice you were hoping for from your real estate agency, it may be time to change your way of marketing.

We have some advertising ideas for social media real estate that will help you maintain high contact with past and potential customers. When a client plans to buy the next home, such tips will help you improve your marketing efforts in social media so that your real estate agency can start to get the attention it deserves and leads.

Tip #1: Stop flooding your followers with irrelevant comments to attract and confuse users on social media. Only posting to hit a certain number of posts per day will not keep your followers engaged; it will make you forgotten.

The key to using social media marketing for real estate effectively is to stick to the 80/20 principle when you make your posts. That means 80% of your posts should be about advice on lifestyle and other aspects of the social interests of your customers, and 20% should be about your real estate agency and what you can sell.

This advice should be easy to follow because you know so much about the communities and activities that hold the attention of your clients as a real estate professional. You'll be able to keep customers engaged because you're talking about their home base, from tips on the best restaurants to the latest home decoration styles, local food classes, and community events.

Tip #2: Invest in Facebook Ads to Generate More Real Estate Leads There are two ways to attract attention through social media for real estate professionals: through organic and paid marketing efforts on social media. Through making the information you post so fascinating and useful that real estate customers want to share it with their social circles, you achieve organic marketing influence through the frequency of your posts. Twitter, Facebook, and other social media channels have changed the way jobs are distributed, making it much harder for real estate agents to reach through organic reach a wide pool of contacts.

That's where it comes into play with paid social marketing. The key to successful lead generation through social media is to ensure that when they are ready to make a sale, your information reaches home buyers and sellers, and Facebook Ads is the perfect way to do that. Facebook ads enable you to target prospective customers based on demographics, topics of interest, and so much more to ensure that the right person sees your ad.

Instead of simply creating a post and hoping to be interested in buying or selling a home from one of your Facebook friends, the specific targeting built into Facebook Ads enables you to reach real estate customers at the exact time they start the home search process.

Tip #3: Focus on the social channels that your real estate customers are following Some realtors are trying to keep up with too many social media channels to reach everyone, and they end up with poor quality posts that attract no one. Each channel of social media marketing has a focus and type of user. For example, LinkedIn is quite popular with business professionals, but it won't connect you to people looking to purchase a home.

Facebook, Twitter, YouTube, and Instagram should focus on winning with the top social media marketing strategies. Such four forms of social media marketing will give you the greatest scope to communicate with property buyers and sellers without running you ragged trying to keep up comments on social sites that won't further your marketing efforts.

Tip #4: Adapt the posts to match the style and color of every social media marketing platform. It's not true that one size fits all when it comes to social media marketing for real estate. If you're trying to use the same post and headline for all your social media marketing strategies for real estate, you'll end up chasing away many potential customers.

Savvy real estate marketers ensure that they adapt their posts ' content to the needs of the audience of each individual social marketing site.

Facebook: Try the tips, style guidelines, and lists for home decoration. Games, quizzes, and competitions are common property posts on Facebook Twitter: the microblogging model suits well with stats and links to real estate data. They are using hashtags to expand the scope of your advertising.

Instagram: Showcase local lifestyles and include short property features tagged with the Photo Map app to let viewers know where to find the homes that feature YouTube: create a dedicated neighborhood tours channel and include clips from your listings.

Tip #5: Incorporate Content to Make the Social Media Marketing Efforts More Successful Marketing and Video in Social Media is a match made in heaven. You can use a single beautiful video of the amazing view of a beach sunset from one of your waterfront listings to boost all your social marketing strategies for real estate.

Show three to ten-second bursts on your Twitter and Facebook updates, use a longer 60-second cut on your Instagram page and view your dedicated YouTube channel's complete glorious video. Taken together, from a single real estate video, that's an amazing amount of social media marketing power!

Consider using Facebook Live Video to promote your next open house for a real marketing boost. Through a live walk-through of the house, take your Facebook followers, and have a Q&A session to answer any questions from curious viewers. It's a great example of how you can use social media marketing strategies to make your marketing efforts offline shine with a little innovation.

Too often, I think, are marketing shortcuts or get-rich-quick schemes obsessed with real estate agents and brokers. The real estate agents will try a plan for a month or two in search of the magic bullet, but if they don't see success, they will drop it and move on. That does not give enough time to gain traction to the marketing strategy, and the constant changes result in an inconsistent message. For sales, it's just a catastrophe formula.

Two or three channels that work well are mastered by the most effective agents. I know that if there was a quick fix, it would be used by everyone. Of course, there are some success stories out there, but they are often misleading. You will find a lot of noise when you actually dive in, but few experts who really know their craft. Start with these five suggestions if you're looking for ways to improve your marketing game and grow your real estate business:

1. Don't neglect paid media.

Google, Facebook, and Instagram ads are worth running, particularly if you're a newer agent. Paid media is perfect for quick lead generation. Usually, our customers see leads within the first week, and cost as low as $3 to $5 per lead has been achieved. These leads, however, still need to be followed up and nurtured in order to become clients. Taking into this strategy can generate leads at low cost, but in order to see a return on investment, continuous follow-up over several months is needed.

2. Recall the SEO isn't gone.

Search engine optimization is still worth exploring for people who are more interested in long-term return on investment. Leads occur organically, but to solidify findings takes a lot longer.

Lead generation is competitive by SEO, and companies must fight to be heard. Google can rate the importance of an organization based on technical optimization, accessibility, and domain authority. It is important to keep a steady stream of potential customers coming to your site with fresh content. Clicks— or the lack of clicks— is instant feedback on how audiences interact with your marketing strategy.

Focus on hyperlocal content to increase the chances of interest generated by your website. A blog post about the area's 10 best restaurants or a business study is doing well because no one else had insights.

3. Concentrate on quality over quantity.

Many agents pay attention to Instagram, which makes sense because of the real estate's visual appeal. Today, the software is only used by 39 percent of real estate companies, and even those who often use it don't do it well.

When posting to Instagram, the most common problems seen that real estate agents are using low-resolution pictures, failing to use hashtag analysis, superimposing too much text over the images, not maintaining a clear visual identity, and not producing enough story articles.

It's so critical to get every detail right in the real estate market. You need to know what looks good and what with buyers and sellers resonates visually. It like more than just user experience: it's about your brand, and you're communicating through your posts.

4. Let it be your guide to analytics.

Marketing analytics provides businesses with a wealth of data, ranging from results-driven metrics to behavioral information. You can improve its effectiveness and boost your return on investment by evaluating the quality of your plan.

Collecting this data would allow you to see and track patterns, identify successful strategies, and forecast outcomes for future efforts. Measure and evaluate your online commitment information and let them direct your marketing strategies. Defining what channels do best, then concentrating on those and mastering them.

5. Plan and stick to it.

There is no development of a successful marketing campaign overnight. Nearly half of the real estate companies are struggling to learn new technologies and use them as part of their overall marketing strategies.

I don't think many agents understand the effort it takes to do differentiated marketing, which is the ultimate outcome. Whether you're generating leads through newsletters, Instagram videos, or paid ads, getting a nursing program in place is important.

The process of real estate sales is long, and it will take some time for any marketing strategies you try to show results. But you will eventually create more business by sticking with a consistent message in the long run.

4.4 Real Estate Digital Marketing Improvements

Real estate digital marketing must tackle its own unique challenges. Nevertheless, just as other businesses have developed highly specialized strategies, it can also be successfully done for real estate.

If you're a real estate agent, the name of the game is competition. Anything in the market that will give you an edge will only increase your earning potential. It may seem daunting to achieve your goals by non-traditional means in a time-honored and well-established industry. Careful strategic planning will be required. But with the undivided population on the internet, the only logical next step is digital real estate marketing.

Salesmanship is all in the real estate industry. Marketing should be an addition of your skillset, no matter what your concept of salesmanship is. Adapting to the advertising landscape's digital change should be a priority when fine-tuning the art.

You are already acquainted with your local competition as a real estate agent. You know you're catering to a demographic of individuals who will become planned house buyers. You also know that your business plan depends on your community knowledge and how you're investing in putting yourself out there.

What you should be mindful of is that many people flock to do their own research online. A revolution has occurred in the conventional model with the proliferation of listing facilities and home scouting sites. In the current landscape, you must fight harder than ever for a customer's business.

Now while this may not be news like yourself to a seasoned real estate agent, keeping up with trends in digital real estate marketing in an ongoing process of development. Trends are organic entities that are constantly moving forward.

The move to the online medium won't require a full tear-down of what you think is true in advertising. Moreover, you just need to understand the future of new tools and philosophies.

That's why we're here to help guide the creation of a successful digital marketing strategy for real estate.

Being concise means the difference between' driving business growth' and' generating prospective leads at my local level.' Vague targets don't do you any favors, so find out exactly what you're trying to achieve.

It is another important factor to describe the priorities by being tangible, both in time and business metrics. Unrealistic goals are seldom achieved. In their industry, everyone wants to be successful, especially in a highly competitive industry such as real estate. To help combat this, take your tactic with a magnifying glass and switch ' generating prospective leads in my locale' to' generating 10 prospective leads this month in my locale.' Real estate agents know it best: you are the product.

What is a better way to set up your brand, you will not only use your social media strategy to interact with your real and digital community, but other sources will also turn to social media to discover more about your potential real estate agent?

Your clients are engaged on social media platforms like Facebook, LinkedIn, Twitter, etc. It doesn't matter what kind of real estate agent you are. You will gain credibility by having a social media presence by being able to connect a real person to your business. It will also help you gain traction on multiple platforms through content marketing.

Here are a handful of tips for online real estate advertising on social media: educating your consumers through value blog articles Chatting directly with your fans to listen to their opinions Promote your family, not just yourself.

Sharing videos on the internet, once viewed by social media, people are much more likely to watch videos. It's even better to live video.

Virtual reality and virtual reality are two of the latest technologies that you can use when you're in the real estate industry. On the other hand, virtual reality gives users a 360-degree view. Both provide a quick view and virtual tour to potential buyers, thus increasing their chances of converting.

Having active social media accounts will boost your online presence, which will do wonders for the search engine optimization of your website.

Build buyer profiles: buyer profiles are the ideal customers through your content that you are trying to target. From new homeowners to current agents, take time to map out who your target is, what they are doing, their average salary, and other features that may affect their decision-making processes.

Start posting relevant content: Whether on your website or in your brokerage, high-value content attracts readers and builds your credibility as a well-informed online expert. Try updating your business blog once a week, including valuable content for a variety of buyer profiles.

Work to improve your SEO: It's not as hard as you might imagine raising your rankings on the search engine results pages of sites like Google and Bing. Take a few minutes a week to review popular and industry-related keywords on Google Ads and make sure they are included in any copy that you develop.

Investment in digital marketing training: Digital marketing skills are becoming increasingly important in running a successful business in the modern marketplace. When deciding to invest in training in digital marketing, you will make sure you have the necessary skills to stand out from your competition. Learn the tools and technologies required by a Certified Diploma in Digital Marketing to address tomorrow's challenges.

Using digital social media marketing is a great way for real estate agents to grow their business as they can connect instantly with existing customers, potential customers, and their companions. While every real estate agent should practice some sort of social media to promote their business, if you do it correctly, this type of marketing will only be successful. Knowing how to leverage social media power to help build your real estate business will enable you to spend your time updating your different social media accounts efficiently.

Building your credibility, the main reason real estate agents need to use social media websites to promote their business is building their reputation. If you can put yourself as an industry expert, attracting new customers will be much easier. Providing informative, high-quality content to your Twitter followers or Facebook fans is the best way to put yourself as an industry expert.

You want to think about your followers that either they will find this information useful. This will maintain consistency with your readers interested and engaged as they look forward to the next source of information you share about the real estate industry.

Network Another reason for real estate professionals to benefit from social media websites is networking within the real estate industry. Reaching through your Facebook page to your current and past customers is a great way to ask for referrals for your business. You may want to encourage your readers to share your article or link to someone they know who is searching for a new house at the end of your posts. A highly effective way to create a new business strategy is to use social media to network with your current and past clients.

Websites on social media are also a great way to network with your peers. Following the Twitter accounts and Facebook pages of other real estate agents is a wonderful way to see how other real estate agents are marketing their business. You can also connect with these real estate agents to ask them any questions about their company through different social media channels. Aligning with other successful real estate agents will also enable you in the industry to thrive.

Diversify your marketing efforts, the more you market your real estate business, the higher your chances of success. Mixing online advertising with social media marketing will help the company reach new customers that traditional methods of marketing would never have reached. Regularly checking your Twitter and Facebook pages is a good way to keep potential customers up to date on your current listings. Another great way to advertise your business in a new way is to upload videos to YouTube. Something as easy as a video slide show posted on YouTube will help you spread the word about your new listing. It's a great way to stimulate their interest in the house by being able to show prospective homebuyers' footage of a new home you've got for sale.

Finding new and inventive ways to market your real estate business, especially in this tough housing market, will help your business thrive. Using different websites for social media is an excellent way to reach new customers and promote your online real estate business.

The average homebuyer is online: 44 percent of homebuyers first searched for online properties, and 83 percent of all homebuyers looking for homes using the internet. Not only that but on a mobile device, 58 percent of all home buyers found their home! Not only do you need to conquer the internet in all the ways they spend their time communicating with these digital, online customers, but you also need to connect with them at every point of their home-buying journey.

The way to do this is through a robust marketing strategy for real estate which claims and leverages all the digital real estate— from search engines to directory listings such as Zillow. See the marketing services that you should include in your online marketing strategy below and if you are willing to sell more properties.

Conclusion:

It is important to create a long-term plan when creating a brand. All brand marketing strategies should guide by enterprise vision, target audience determination, consistency creation, and emotion communication.

Advances in technology and the power of the Internet have changed the playing field for most of us, so if you want to stand out from the crowd, the need for an innovative and successful marketing plan is more critical than ever. In order to get your real estate career started, a real estate brand identity is not only an important aspect but a powerful tool to succeed. Yet brand identity is more than just bright icons and clever slogans— it is a commitment to the promise of your customer.

You need to consider each target audience's context and the niche in which you will be operating. Here are a few demographics and the importance of considering each when deciding on your brand: residents of any property you buy need to trust you as a buyer, and, most importantly, you need to understand how to find and engage with prospective tenants and provide satisfactory customer service.

As much as the corporate strategy must compensate for the advertising strategy, marketing also must ensure that they work on the various aspects of product packaging, design, etc. and continue to work on the brand so that it is compatible with the changing times, markets, consumer expectations, and taste, etc. A certain product or business' market dominance and competitiveness are realized through the brand value. Maintaining brand leadership calls for long-term strategic planning.

References:

Medium. (2019). Actionable Real Estate Marketing Ideas for 2020. [online] Available at: https://medium.com/@NakulChandra/actionable-real-estate-marketing-ideas-for-2020-ac454148c4fc.

Digital Marketing Institute. (2019). 8 Ways Realtors Can Use Digital Marketing to Boost Sales. [online] Available at: https://digitalmarketinginstitute.com/en-us/blog/8-ways-realtors-can-use-digital-marketing-to-boost-sales.

Gensleron.com. (2019). Real Estate Marketing: The Allure of a Lifestyle Brand - Lifestyle Strategy and Design - architecture and design. [online] Available at: http://www.gensleron.com/lifestyle/2015/2/10/real-estate-marketing-the-allure-of-a-lifestyle-brand.html.

Eplattenier, E. (2019). The Ultimate Guide to Real Estate Branding. [online] Fit Small Business. Available at: https://fitsmallbusiness.com/real-estate-branding/

Stitcher.com. (2019). 670: Outperform the Competition in Any Real Estate Market with Aleksandra Scepanovic from Real Estate Rockstars. [online] Available at: https://www.stitcher.com/podcast/hiban-digital/pat-hiban-interviews-real-estate-rockstars/e/55123099.

Williams, J. (2019). The Basics of Branding. [online] Entrepreneur. Available at:

https://www.entrepreneur.com/article/77408.

It, B. (2019). Why Brand Identity Matters and How to Build It Better. [online] Business News Daily. Available at: https://www.businessnewsdaily.com/2044-steps-branding.html.

ScrapeHero. (2019). Brand Monitoring - How to monitor your brand on the Internet. [online] Available at: https://www.scrapehero.com/brand-monitoring/.

Sooper Articles. (2019). Real Estate and The Importance of Digital Marketing. [online] Available at: https://www.sooperarticles.com/real-estate-articles/real-estate-importance-digital-marketing-1744301.html.

Co-Communications. (2019). Five essentials for building a real estate brand - Co-Communications. [online] Available at: https://cocommunications.com/2014/10/27/five-essentials-building-real-estate-brand/.